Niall Breslin is a retired professional athlete, composer, author, documentary-maker, campaigner and multi-award-winning social entrepreneur and podcaster, currently completing a PhD at Trinity College Dublin. His acclaimed podcast *Where Is My Mind?* has featured global wellness leaders and led to further work including the hugely popular *Wake Up / Wind Down* podcast on Spotify, and appearances on BBC Radio 3 Unwind and Audible (the investigative podcast *The Madman's Hotel*), all reflecting his deep commitment to progressing the systems and conversations on the human condition in the chaos of the modern world.

ALSO BY NIALL BRESLIN
Non-fiction
Me and my Mate Jeffrey

Children's
The Magic Moment
Take Five
The Chill Skill
The Sleep Scan

The Place That Has Never Been Wounded

A mindful journey home to yourself

NIALL BRESLIN

First published in Great Britain by John Murray One in 2026
An imprint of John Murray Group

1

Copyright © Niall Breslin 2026

The right of Niall Breslin to be identified as the Author of the Work has been asserted by him in accordance with the Copyright, Designs and Patents Act 1988.

'The Facts of Life' © Pádraig Ó Tuama, 2013

All rights reserved. No part of this publication may be reproduced, stored in a retrieval system, or transmitted, in any form or by any means without the prior written permission of the publisher, nor be otherwise circulated in any form of binding or cover other than that in which it is published and without a similar condition being imposed on the subsequent purchaser.

A CIP catalogue record for this title is available from the British Library

Trade Paperback ISBN 978 1 399 82368 5
ebook ISBN 978 1 399 82369 2

Typeset in Bembo MT by Hewer Text UK Ltd, Edinburgh
Printed and bound in Great Britain by Clays Ltd, Elcograf S.p.A.

John Murray Group policy is to use papers that are natural, renewable and recyclable products and made from wood grown in sustainable forests. The logging and manufacturing processes are expected to conform to the environmental regulations of the country of origin.

John Murray Group	John Murray One
Carmelite House	Hachette Book Group
50 Victoria Embankment	123 South Broad Street
London EC4Y 0DZ	Ste 2750
	Philadelphia, PA 19109, USA

www.johnmurraypress.co.uk

John Murray Group, part of Hodder & Stoughton Limited
An Hachette UK company

The authorised representative in the EEA is Hachette Ireland, 8 Castlecourt Centre, Dublin 15, D15 XTP3, Ireland (email: info@hbgi.ie)

To Louise, Stevie, Mum, Dad, Ronan, Laura, Julie, Andrea, Billy and Caelan.

And to all those who have offered wisdom and humanity out to the world to make it a better place for us all. We need you now more than ever.

This book was penned from a place of genuine feeling. Each chapter has been carefully crafted to reinforce the central themes and message through storytelling, metaphors and insights drawn from my experiences in mindfulness and life. The stories are told as I remember them, not as exact accounts, but as reflections meant to convey their essence and emotional truth. My hope is that you find within them a sense of connection, relatability and inspiration to apply these reflections to your own experiences and personal view of the world.

Contents

Notes on the audio	ix
Prologue	1
ACT I	**15**
Introduction: The Polaris Principles	17
Chapter 1: Non-Judgement	29
Chapter 2: Untethering	41
Chapter 3: The Novice Soul	55
Chapter 4: The Credence Frequency	71
Chapter 5 : Grace	83
ACT II	**95**
Introduction: Dúchas	97
Chapter 6: Be the Lake	107
Chapter 7: Be the Mountain	119
Chapter 8: Be the Sky	133
Chapter 9: Be the Beauty	147
Chapter 10: Be Your Truth	157
ACT III	**171**
Introduction: Metta	173
Chapter 11: The Midday Moon	183
Chapter 12: The Facts of Life	197
Chapter 13: Loving-kindness	211

ACT IV	227
Introduction: The Place That Has Never Been Wounded	229
Notes	241
Acknowledgements	243

Notes on the audio

This book is accompanied by a soundtrack – a collection of compositions and guided reflections/meditations that relate to the theme and sentiment of each chapter.

When I was a child, after my grandfather Bumper passed away, his Bechstein piano made its way from Glasgow to our home in Mullingar. It no longer fit in my grandmother's flat, so it found a new life in our front room. The day it arrived, I was mesmerised. I sat behind it for hours, teaching myself to play – not because I wanted lessons (my mum, a classically trained violinist and pianist, gave plenty of those at home), but because I wanted to embody it.

For me, the piano has always been more than an instrument. It's a voice. It's an extension of human conversation, speaking all the things we struggle to say out loud. It became a higher form of communication, a language of emotion and presence.

I wanted that to be part of this journey for you, too. So, I composed fourteen pieces of music to accompany each chapter. They represent the spirit and essence behind the ideas that guide us towards that quiet place within us that has never been wounded.

The guided meditations and reflections were built around the music to deepen the experience, to carry you when you need carrying, to soothe you when you need soothing and to guide you when you feel a little lost.

THE PLACE THAT HAS NEVER BEEN WOUNDED

You can listen in whatever way feels right alongside each chapter, all at once, or by choosing the pieces that call to you in any given moment. I hope that they bring you exactly what you need, exactly when you need it.

Prologue

I could hear my dad opening a can of beer downstairs as he went through his usual Tuesday-evening ritual of cooking dinner for my mother, who was in the sitting room watching *Grand Designs* with a reasonably grand gin and tonic. Drive-time radio was blaring at a decibel level akin to the main stage at Glastonbury as Dad cooked his steaks in a bath of butter (despite our pointless protests, given the quadruple bypass he'd had a few years previously). My dad, God bless him, is an ex-military man, and his auditory perception wasn't what it used to be. But I will come back to that one.

There was nothing my dad loved more than these simple moments of culinary circumspection, and once they made him happy, they made me happy. Upstairs, I lay on my childhood bedroom bed (which I had long grown out of), staring out the window at the fading light of an autumn evening, the opening act of the darkness of an Irish winter.

I had my first panic attack in that room, when I was 14 years of age. It was as if somebody walked into my bedroom and put a pillow over my face; I tore the sheets, trying to find a breath; every cell in my body believed I was dying. The image of myself in the mirror with blood-red eyes and a heart trying to punch its way out of my chest is as vivid today as it was in 1994.

It was never the same after that. I remember thinking I might be possessed – a viable option in the 1990s in Ireland. I then looked for answers in the most terrifying book ever penned: not the Bible, but *The Encyclopaedia of Health*. It had every disease known to men and women within its pages, and long before we used Google to diagnose our every ailment, we consulted this thing. On a Monday, I would have appendicitis; on Tuesday, I would have cancer; and by Wednesday, I would be pregnant. I talked myself into every disease in this book until, one day, I saw the word 'asthma'. *That's it – that's what's wrong with me.* Relief flushed through my body that I had discovered the reason I was suffocating on my bed most nights.

I told my parents that I thought I might have asthma. They sent me to the doctor, who informed me that it wasn't asthma; that it was, indeed, puberty. Now, I know things get weird, and things grow, and you can't watch *Baywatch* with your parents any more, but you can breathe. In my heart, I knew it was not asthma. A muted hope lingered that the doctor would offer me an answer.

It takes deep, unsettling courage to present yourself to a medical professional without an obvious ailment to point to, no broken bone, no fever, no rash. You brace yourself for the possibility of not being believed or, worse, being dismissed entirely. And that dismissal set me on an utterly destructive path. There is a profound loneliness in fighting an inner war when those meant to be your allies turn their backs on you.

Adulthood, thankfully, brought a different story. The polar opposite of my past struggles, my experience in seeking help as an adult was met not with dismissal but with understanding, compassion, and the steady hand of guidance. In my doctors, I found not just care, but a steadying solace, a place where empathy replaced uncertainty, and healing became more than a possibility and a vacuous inspirational meme.

A little while before this, my family and I had moved to the Middle East to be close to my dad, who was serving as a peacekeeper with the United Nations in Lebanon. There had been relative peace in the Middle East for almost a decade – until the day the Breslins arrived. What is now referred to as Operation Accountability or the 'Seven-Day War' started between the Israel Defence Forces and Hezbollah in southern Lebanon, where many civilians lost their lives, and where we were staying was slap-bang in the middle of it, in a town called Nahariya in northern Israel.

We had not been there that long when, in the middle of the night, I was woken by women with broken English on megaphones encouraging us to get into our bomb shelters. The apartment walls vibrated menacingly from the shells dropping just a few miles up the road. IDF fighter jets tore past overhead. I will never forget the noise of those engines. They sounded like death.

Growing up in Ireland, I had witnessed violence throughout the 1980s on our television screens, only 50 to 60 miles away from where I was from, but it still felt far away. This war could not have felt closer. My dad, an incredibly experienced military man, was on his third tour of duty to this part of the world. He did his very best to assure me that we were safe: 'Go back to sleep, son.'

His inane attempt at comfort didn't go down well. '"Go back to sleep," Da?' There are fucking bombs dropping up the road, warships in the harbour, and fighter jets breaking sound barriers over our heads. I will stay very much fucking awake if it's all right with you.

A switch flicked on in me that night and has never turned off. I am not really into labels. You can call it post-traumatic stress disorder or whatever you want, but I, for one, think it was a perfectly healthy reaction to the shitshow that is a front-row seat of war. In later years, when I started to do some digging into my psychology, I came to believe in the Middle East was just the catalyst. A dormant anxiety had lived within me for as long as I can remember.

I went to a primary school in my hometown that the Christian Brothers ran. What went on there has never left me. In my first class in primary school, I watched my teacher beat a traveller kid so viciously that I physically shook for days after it. The teacher was almost foaming at the mouth as he battered the leather strap across this child's hand, which was swelling with every strike. After the beating, this kid sat beside me and put his cold metal pencil case on his hands to try and soothe the pain. This abuse was just the beginning of what was to come. Over the next six years, the beatings were regular, and I was at the receiving end of quite a few of them. I remember being hit in the back of the neck with the tip of a fishing rod because my foot was on a chair. I was on crutches then, so I had to keep my foot elevated. There was also a lot of bullying. I don't blame anyone for that. We were surrounded by violence, and, often, we just turned it on each other. Unfortunately, there was also sexual abuse. One of my teachers served a lengthy jail term for multiple sexual offences against some of my peers.

I hated that place. But to survive it, I adapted, becoming chronically hypervigilant. I always expected violence, so my entire central nervous system was stuck in fight or flight for six to seven hours a day. I cut myself off emotionally, as I would rather feel nothing than feel everything.

This adaptive child haunted me throughout my adulthood. I found it hard to connect or be intimate. But I was one of the lucky ones because I got to go home, where I experienced love and safety, apart from the occasional sibling riot. And I carried this with me to the Middle East, as well as the nuclear hormone bomb that is puberty. It was a perfect storm.

Then came 9 April 1994. I was walking into school in a daze after a shit night's sleep, thanks to a belter of a panic attack. I went into the Topic, a local newsagent, and saw a picture of my hero on the front of the paper. The headline said, 'Kurt Cobain dead'. It was as if someone punched me in the chest. I felt physically sick, in a state of utter shock, mirroring that feeling back in my bedroom in Nahariya. I stumbled numbly into school, unable to speak. When I finally got the nerve to open my mouth, I asked the teacher what had happened. He was well aware that the class worshipped Kurt Cobain. He punched his desk and screamed, 'Coward!' That was my mental health education.

My teenage years were a paradox of fuckedupness and, despite it all, success. I represented my county in football and my province and country in rugby, but behind it all, it was chaos. A hedonistic cocktail of self-harm, insomnia, panic attacks and a rogue mind torturing me any time it got me on its own.

I got a rugby scholarship to attend University College Dublin, where I studied economics, sociology and psychology. My first day was spent in the toilets of the arts block, drowning in sweat, vomit and tears. A panic attack had greeted me like a kick in the face after entering my first lecture. I got used to these toilet rendezvous. I used to take great solace in reading the witty and often charming notes sketched into the doors and walls by those in a reflective moment while relieving themselves. (Sadly, that is not the case any more, as people are too busy scrolling their hand-held prison while taking a dump than to gift future toilet pilgrims with their sage seeds of carefully chiselled enlightenment – a true casualty of modernity.)

I acted my way through university. I was selected to represent the Ireland under-21 rugby squad in Sydney at the 2001 World Cup. Most nights, I would sleep with a pillow over my face so my roommate wouldn't hear me gasping for air. But I played every minute of every game, and when I returned, I was offered a full-time professional contract with one of the top teams in Europe: Leinster Rugby.

At this stage, I was in the arms of darkness. I was experiencing bouts of depression that left me blitzed. I still have not come up with, or read, a definition that can accurately describe depression. It wasn't a sadness but a nothingness, a quest for feeling with no map or even point of direction. I would take a handful of Xanax before games, terrified that I would be drug-tested (hardly a performance-enhancing drug, but still). Every Monday, I would go in for my medical and promise myself I would tell the doctor what was happening, but I didn't even have the language to describe it. I would miss training sessions and tell my coach I had to get my wisdom teeth removed. I must have been the only human on earth whose wisdom teeth grew back, as it was my go-to excuse on many occasions.

And then my body gave up on me. Two and a half years later, I announced my retirement. I asked my coach at the time, Matt Williams, onto my podcast a few years back, and asked him what he had thought was wrong with me. He said, 'We felt you were an alcoholic, and you didn't care.' I respect his honesty, but it hurt. Most nights, I still have a recurring dream of getting to a rugby pitch to play a game and forgetting one item, like my boots or gumshield. My subconscious is not ready to let go. Unfinished business can cling on to the psyche like chewing gum in a good head of hair.

That was the start of my music career. Sport was what I did; music is what I am. Every cell in my body reverberates with music. At the time, I never had the guts to commit to it as a profession. Even though my mother was a musician and my brother a producer, I was told enough times in school that it was what 'wasters' do. One teacher in secondary school took particular delight in telling me that. (By the by, I went to the same school as Niall Horan from One Direction. I do wonder if that teacher ever told him the same thing.) But music suited me better; you were expected to be miserable and shoe gazey, so it fit my brand.

PROLOGUE

It did not take long before the band was signed to Universal Records, and the Oasis management even flirted with us. We had quite the journey. Supporting AC/DC, Bon Jovi and Oasis along the way; platinum albums, tours and debauchery that only the road can bring. But once again, my self-sabotaging addiction to carnage put an end to that. If I am honest, it broke my heart. For when you are the one who wields the blade that cuts your own heart, the pain takes on a haunting, almost Shakespearean weight; a tragedy where the villain and the victim are one and the same.

London came calling amid grief. I was signed as a songwriter to Universal Music Publishing and 19 Entertainment, home of the Spice Girls and David Beckham. Moving to London, I was half expecting people to sing to me as I came in through the arrivals area of Heathrow, or to see Hugh Grant walking around Notting Hill, but the reality was somewhat different. Skint and living in the arse-end of east Putney, being that weird, country Irish lad who says hello to everyone on the street (heads up, don't say hello to everyone on the street in London, or you'll end up in a psychiatric facility) and experiencing the wrath of a rush-hour underground journey in a train you do not fit in while being tutted at by people stuck under your armpit, is not exactly a Richard Curtis movie.

One thing that is never that far around the corner when you are internalising and repressing pain is addiction. I was hyper-aware of addiction. No matter how fucked up things got, I was determined it would never capture me. But that is not how addiction works. It waits till you have no defences left, and then it just swans in like a bad guy coming into a saloon in a Western. My weapon of choice was sleeping pills. I was consuming them like mints. I was battling severe insomnia in London, which was literally driving me insane: I could sense the sanity leaving me with each sleepless night. The sleeping pills were the lesser of two evils, but it did not take long before I was robbing scripts from doctors' surgeries and pleading with pharmacies to sort me out. My addiction started to manifest physically. I began to lose my hair, and I would sweat so profusely that I would have to bring a change of clothes when meeting up with mates.

There was a real sense that I was losing the plot. Sure enough, a dark night of the soul, or whatever you want to call it, came, and it was fucking devastating. I will never forget the terror. There is a particular horror that comes with the belief that you have lost your mind. Your world becomes so small, so out of focus.

I got help that night. It was the most critical decision I had ever made.

Not long after this, I got offered a new job as a coach on the highly successful TV series *The Voice of Ireland*. I wasn't sure if this was the right move, but I was skint. I could not even afford to fly home, and I missed my family a lot. (As depressed as I was, I wasn't prepared to do the Holyhead ferry route to Dublin. You are either eight hours early or eight hours late for the ferry, and the Irish Sea is generally like an episode of *Deadliest Catch*.)

The production company said they would fly me home weekly, so I went for it. But all that went through my head from the minute I signed that contract was, *You are going to have a panic attack on live television.* It was a relentless anthem. Right enough, ten minutes before live TV for the biggest show in the country, our stage manager was banging on my dressing room door, screaming at me to get miked and get side of stage. Behind the door, I was gasping for air, retching on vomit, tears pissing down my face as I viciously shook on the floor, my carefully pressed shirt ripping at the collar in my attempt to catch a breath.

After what felt like an hour, but was probably only a minute or two later, I stood up and looked in the mirror. *It's over now,* I thought. *I can't hide this.* For those unaware, men wear make-up on television (for the shine, apparently). I looked like I had been dumped at my grad ball.

I do not know where my strength came from that night, but it has clarified one thing. This behaviour is not a weakness; we are not broken or powerless. People who deal with this are some of the most influential and strong people on this earth. Because I do not know many people who would have been able to get themselves out of the hole I was in that night, walk out onto prime-time TV, and pretend everything was all right. (Though to be fair, I had a lot of training at it.)

I don't remember that show. I look back at it, and I do not recognise myself. Once the end credits rolled, I got into a taxi, returned to my hotel room and collapsed. I sobbed for hours; I only stopped because I got so dehydrated there were no tears left in me.

When you hit rock bottom, you have two choices: stay there, or find a way out.

In my experience, I see more in the dark. A clarity of self-awareness often comes when you are at your most vulnerable. It's like an opportunity presents itself. My good friend and mentor, Michael Harding, once told me that depression is like a point of growth, because we are letting go of that part of ourselves that doesn't serve us any more. But I think about it slightly differently. I don't want to let go of that side of myself. It is part of me and the culmination of my life experiences. I tried to get to know that familiar stranger. I did not want to run away from him any more. You often hear folks say you should not make significant decisions at times of heightened emotion. That is a load of bollocks. These moments can be revolutionary catalysts for change. Lying on the hotel room floor, I experienced a coherency that had not visited me in many years. I made two decisions that would ultimately change the trajectory of my life and lead me on a path stranger than fiction.

The first decision was to speak publicly about my experience over the last two decades. I thought of the 14-year-old me sitting in my classroom after Kurt Cobain died, utterly lost and shamed. What words did I need to hear that day? What would have made me feel less alone? I didn't want young people going through this sort of shit, thinking they are broken. I wanted to give them the language to express themselves – the language that felt so foreign to me and my friends growing up. I also knew I needed to take the power away from the public. I could not mute or numb myself any more. My behaviour was heavily influenced by other people's perceptions of who I was. When you do prime-time entertainment TV, there is a sense that people have ownership over who you are. That becomes even more overwhelming when you don't have a fucking clue who you are. There was a risk to this, but no one was talking about it. As prevalent as it is now in cultural discourse, it was non-existent 12 years ago.

I accepted that I would lose my job and have to leave the country. (Catastrophising has always been one of my most impressive cognitive skills.)

The other decision I made that night was to name my mind. I called him Jeffrey. 'Listen, Jeffrey, this is not working for either of us,' I said to the end of the bed, questioning my sanity, not for the first time in my life. Humanising the cognitive chaos that had battered me my whole life made it somewhat tangible and more real. I took out three pieces of hotel paper and wrote on one piece of paper everything Jeffrey liked, on another everything he didn't like, and then finally everything we had to do to figure out why we were kicking the living shit out of each other every day. It was that simple.

PROLOGUE

The lists are unimportant, apart from what I was going to do. I got a new doctor, Neil Healy. He was the trendy new GP in town that all the mothers fancied. My mum would ask, 'Did you go to see him? What's he like?' God help the guy, but I talked to him for over an hour. I purged myself. But for the first time, I felt fully contained and held by a health professional. He was honest about what lay ahead of me: 'You've got to show up in therapy.'

I did not know what he meant, but I do now. He meant the scenic route, a longer journey, crap roads and hills – but the view was worth it. What I learned on the way transformed my life in a way that feels almost unrecognisable from what I experienced in the past. And I'm telling you all this because I need you to know that what you are about to read is not a lecture. I do not speak from an elevated position; I talk to you as your peer and fellow human trying to navigate the shitshow of life.

But let's return to my childhood bedroom, where I started this story. As I lay on the bed, I put on my headphones and took my first step towards mindfulness meditation – after finally heeding the well-intentioned and incessant encouragement of my more awakened friends and colleagues.

There is an array of definitions for mindfulness. The most commonly used is 'paying attention to the present moment without judgement'. (I sometimes like to define it as stepping into an ice-cold shower – the minute the water cuts the arse off you, tell me if you're worrying about yesterday or what you have to do tomorrow! But my colleagues haven't entirely warmed to that one.) In a world high on information, we often seek out complex and convoluted explanations and dismiss the mundane and obvious ones. I advocate embracing the simplicity of this definition, but frequently, the simplest of explanations come with the most significant challenges. The modern world has conditioned us to be anything but mindful. In fact, for many of us, sitting down and focusing our awareness on our body or breath has become a genuinely testing endeavour.

And I was nervous. I found it challenging to focus on my breath, as that was the core manifestation of my panic attacks. Sitting still for longer than a minute without my skin crawling was impossible. My central nervous system would cramp. I was also immensely embarrassed at the idea of meditation. I don't know why I was so allergic to the concept of it. I used to get pissed off with well-intentioned people telling me to meditate, as if it was the panacea to every possible ailment that existed. I also equated spirituality with religion. And organised religion had quite literally beaten any spirituality I had out of me.

Nobody could know I was exploring this. I pressed 'play' on the audio link. It started with a voice halfway between angelic and creepy, a stock ambient track with trickling water that annoyingly always triggers my need to pee (I have the bladder of a 95-year-old). But then something strange started to happen. I sensed an ease filter through my chest. My typically shallow breath deepened and slowed. The chaos and carnage that ruled my mind were replaced with a clearing. There was an acceptance of the experience and a letting go of the need to control.

I don't say this lightly, but I was beginning to relax.

Dimly, I could hear the muffled sound of someone coming up the stairs. Mum was probably coming up to turn on the heating. The steps were coming towards my room. My serene state now disturbed, my central nervous system reverted to type. My dad knocked on my bedroom door to inform me that dinner was ready, dragging me from the first sense of peace I had experienced without drugs or alcohol in 20 years. Like a petulant child, I screamed, 'I AM MEDITATING!'

My dad thought I said something else. As I mentioned, Dad's hearing is not what it used to be.

Ten minutes later, sitting at the kitchen table, I thought about smoothing the situation. 'Da, can you pass the sauce?'

He couldn't look me in the eye.

It was less embarrassing for me to let Dad believe that I was, you know . . . than to tell him I was meditating. I thought there was less explanation involved.

So, if you are reading this, Dad, I would like to confirm, for the record:

I WAS *MEDITATING*.

Act I

The Polaris Principles

The North Star, Polaris, is not merely a distant light scattered on the fabric of the night sky. It is a symbol, a benchmark, a guiding hand stretched across time. For centuries, Polaris has served as a beacon for those navigating through life's upheavals, when the world feels as if it's unravelling, when the familiar is stripped away, leaving only the unknown. While other stars drift with the Earth's restless turning, Polaris remains steadfast, a fixed point in the chaos, whispering assurances of direction to those who require it. And isn't that what we all seek? A constant when all else falters, a still centre when the ground beneath us shifts? In a world so often elusive with uncertainty, we long for a marker, something to anchor, orient and remind us of where we are and, perhaps, who we are (at the risk of sounding like a moment of reflection in a Hallmark movie).

But Polaris is not just a celestial compass: it is also a reminder that direction exists even when it cannot be seen, even when the world is cloaked in darkness. Polaris reminds us that true direction isn't something we chase across the stars but discover patiently within ourselves. It tells us that we possess an internal North Star in our darkest moments – an unyielding point of light to navigate by. To find it, we need only trust the stillness and the simple truth that, no matter how fierce the storm, something steady and unshaken remains within us: what Meister Eckhart, the fourteenth-century

German philosopher, referred to as 'a place in the soul where you've never been wounded'.

This book is about using all my creative and personal experience and knowledge to help guide you to that place, through personal stories, academic learnings, carefully constructed sonic soundtracks and spoken-word mindful reflections and meditations that will accompany each chapter. Over the past four years, I have composed and crafted music and soundscapes to accompany this journey – pieces that, for me, echo the spirit, sentiment and direction of the path we are about to walk. Music has always been my truest gateway into mindfulness meditation; in the most challenging chapters of my life, it offered something sacrosanct: a symphony amid the chaos. As Victor Hugo said: 'Music expresses that which cannot be put into words and that which cannot remain silent.'

What you will hear, and I hope, too, what you will *feel*, is my recovery, a journey back to something I thought I had lost. For a time, I drifted from performance, writing and the simple act of sitting at a piano and believing in what my hands could create. Every touch of the keys brought more doubt than music. But in recent years, there has been a reconnection, a gradual rebuilding of confidence, a return to knowing. The music you'll hear carries me back to when it was all new: sitting at my grandfather's Bechstein piano, utterly enchanted by the way hammers striking strings could make the air shimmer with sound. Today, screens and noise often steal children's wonder, but I found mine, long ago, in the sound of that piano. What you'll also hear is music that, at times, felt as if it wrote itself – music that will walk with you, step by step, offering a sanctuary of sound as you make your way towards the untainted, unaffected, steady and consistent part of yourself. The part of yourself that holds steady when the world shakes.

For me, the combination of language, the human voice and music is the most powerful of all healers, and I aim to communicate in three ways: through relatability, I want you to see yourself in my words and stories; through vulnerability, because that moves you from the head into the heart, and that is where change happens; and, finally, through functionality – I want you to have something you can apply to your everyday lives, interactions and relationships.

Very importantly, I don't speak from a place of hierarchy like I have all this figured out and spend my days dancing in nirvana, but I want to talk to you as a fellow human and with all the good, the bad and the ugly that comes with that. But I want you to know you are in safe hands here. I will guide you with care and courage. All I ask for is an open heart and mind, and a little bravery – because it will take that.

To help you find the place that has never been wounded, I will guide you through four acts. This first act of the book concerns the 'Polaris principles' – a set of principles, a north star, to help guide you when you get lost. These five guiding attitudes will help you navigate the journey inwards, sometimes called attitudes of practice, stemming from the work of Jon Kabat-Zinn.

This exploration isn't about discovering something new but remembering something that's always been there.

As Act I unfolds, we step together into a journey that invites us to listen more deeply and reflect more honestly using the principles and guidance of mindfulness, to rediscover a part of ourselves that has remained untainted by the turbulence of life. Mindfulness, however, is not a smooth road leading to a fated destination; it's an uneven, bumpy track that requires patience, attention and emotional flexibility. This practice of turning the awareness inwards is a deliberate act of slowing down in a world that pushes us towards speed, distraction, productivity and constant output. It's not about adding something more; it's about peeling back what no longer serves you. The path inwards winds and weaves; it was never meant to be a straight road. You will lose your way – we all do – and in those moments of wandering, something essential is found. Getting lost is not a detour; it is the way.

The Polaris principles are here to steady you when the ground beneath you feels uncertain, the direction hazy. Some old patterns, life traps and worn-out habits cling to us more than we realise and, here, we are given the space to lay them down and move beyond them. But letting go doesn't mean losing. It means making room. These principles will help you sense the overwhelming moments, bring you back when you drift, and anchor you. They are not rigid rules to follow but steady companions to lean on.

As we begin, I ask only this: approach the journey with openness. Trust that even in moments of doubt or discomfort, a part of you knows the way. These principles are your guide to rediscovering that steady, untouchable core – the place that has never been wounded.

So, what are the Polaris principles? Before we explore them through richer detail and more personal reflection, let me summarise them here.

1. Non-judgement

The first Polaris principle of non-judgement is a cornerstone, and a radical act in a culture so attuned to the very act of judgement. Imagine, if you will, stepping into a boundless landscape of the present moment, unshackled by the weight of critique. It sounds deceptively simple. But the human mind complicates even the purest intentions with its intricate layers and looping narratives. In our external lives, judgement is the currency of interaction. Socially, personally and professionally, we craft ourselves as actors on a stage, rehearsing lines for an audience that may not even be listening. The sociologist Erving Goffman spoke of the presentation of the everyday self.[1] We each carry two versions of ourselves through the world. The front-stage self is the polished actor, carefully lit and scripted, stepping into society's gaze. This is the self we craft to belong, conform and meet the swirling expectations placed upon us. It is not false, but it is, perhaps, incomplete. Behind the curtain, however, waits another self: truer, and often trembling with the weight of its authenticity. This backstage self knows the lines we wish we could say, the truths we long to live. Yet fear – that perennial critic – keeps the curtains drawn. We worry that the applause will stop if the world glimpses this unrehearsed version of us. And so, in essence, we are all actors in a play we did not entirely audition for, hoping that, one day, we might step fully into the light as ourselves.

Still, even Goffman couldn't foresee the dizzying spotlight of social media, where perception is no longer a side effect but a central axis around which we spin. This fear of judgement infiltrates our inner world, too, like a stubborn shadow. It whispers, *'You're not enough. You'll never get it right. Why bother?'*

These are not truths, but echoes of a system that keeps us tethered to self-doubt.

But here's the foundational core of mindfulness: we are not here to battle judgement or cling to it. We are here to let it pass.

As you move towards the unaffected, steady and consistent part of yourself, you will realise that judgement has no seat at this table. It will beg for a fight you don't need to give. So, when judgement arises, and it will, meet it with a gentle awareness. No resistance, no blame. And then, let it go.

In this letting go, you will discover the lightness you've been carrying all along, hidden beneath the heavy costumes we wear for a world obsessed with criticism and performance.

And, over time, the self we show and the self we are become the same.

2. Untethering

We arrive now at our second Polaris principle: untethering, or *the craft of letting go*. After we've begun to grasp and practise non-judgement, this principle invites us to loosen the grip we often place on outcomes and to release the shackles of expectation. When we sit with ourselves and enter our internal world, it's natural to arrive with a purpose – a desire to feel relaxed, content or energised, a yearning to emerge transformed in some way. We clutch at the hope for a positive experience, clinging to moments of ease or bracing ourselves against the possibility of discomfort. We push away the prick of restlessness, distract ourselves and retreat into imagined worlds. This is instinctual, this dance of attachment and aversion. It is deeply human. But life itself is impermanence, a great shifting tide that gives and takes in equal measure. The tighter we hold on to something – pleasure, peace, certainty – the more elusive it can become.

This principle calls us to untether ourselves from desires and the need to control and curate our internal experience. To unshackle from outcomes and be as we are in the exposed immediacy of the moment. On this path, you will encounter beauty that captivates and fears that consume. Let them come. Let them go. Do not make this sacred space another battleground, another place to measure your worth. You have no 'key performance indicator' here, no boxes to tick, and no metrics to meet.

Untethering in mindfulness meditation is not something to conquer or perfect. It's the awareness of the existence of our need to control our internal experience rather than to witness it. It's a reprieve from the relentless striving of the external world

– a space that belongs to you, and you alone. Let go of the need for this to be anything other than what it is. Release yourself from the pendulum of time and the burden of consequences and conclusions. Sink into the present moment, untethered, and discover the freedom in simply being, whatever that may be.

3. *The Novice Soul*

The third Polaris principle concerns 'the novice soul'. Of all the Polaris principles, this one altered my meditation practice, and indeed my everyday life, most strikingly. It gave me back something I thought was long buried beneath the debris of adulthood: wonder.

There's a concept in Taoism: the uncarved block. This is the unaltered, untouched state before life whittles us into shapes. Before we learn to see the world through filters of expectation and exhaustion. This is how we enter the world: as novice souls, curious, absorbing the ordinary as if it were revelation. A child doesn't merely walk; they explore. They don't just see; they witness, with the focus akin to a neurosurgeon while partaking in the most mundane of tasks. Every moment arrives pristine, unburdened by what came before or what might come after. Somewhere along the way, we unlearn this. We mistake jadedness for wisdom and hurry for purpose. But that original way of being, that uncarved presence, never truly leaves us. It lingers in the edges of our attention, waiting to be rediscovered.

But as we age, the contours of what we value shift and settle. What once felt earth-shatteringly important during the feverish obsessions of childhood and youth gradually fades into irrelevance as we plunge headfirst into the tangled labyrinth of adulthood. And with the passing years, something more consequential can slip away too, almost unnoticed: the capacity to be awestruck. Wonder, that vital, luminous thread that tied us to the world, slowly dissolves. In its place comes the convenience of omnipresence, 24/7 access to a world compressed into the three-second flicker of a swipe. Once expansive and alive, curiosity shrinks to fit the dimensions of a screen, and with it, a potential to be entertained by a performing world.

Yet, now and then, wonder breaches the surface. A moment so vivid, so unexpectedly electric, grips you and reminds you of what it means to feel alive. It is the sensation of being a child again, standing on the precipice of discovery, when every leaf, every bird, every playground was an uncharted dimension worth exploring. Breakfast could be an odyssey; a cardboard box a portal; the faces of our loved ones the worlds around which our tiny, eager orbits revolved.

But life hardens us. It moves us towards other pursuits: achievement, wealth, status – the glittering, false 'wonders' of adulthood.

The novice soul erodes under the weight of practicality, of routine. However, what mindfulness asks of us is simple: to return to that curiosity, to rediscover the beginner's mind with which we once entered the world. When we bring this novice soul into our mindfulness practice, something remarkable happens. We explore every sensation and every emotion, not with the weary knowingness of experience but with the cradling curiosity of encountering it, as if it's the first time. The heavy becomes lighter. The joy becomes richer. The mundane becomes sacred. The novice soul becomes a rebellion against the stale predictability of modern life.

Each breath is an invitation to start again. Each moment is unrepeatable. Each emotion becomes a teacher. And so we tread this path, not with the weight of judgement or expectation, but with the lightness of curiosity. With wonder. With a novice soul.

4. The Credence Frequency

I once found myself searching for a way to articulate the silent, effervescent partnership between the body and the mind. From that search emerged the word 'credence', and so the fourth principle received its name. It's more than a term: it's a knowing; an undeniable truth; a clarity that dissolves doubt. A purity of signal that is untainted by static or distraction.

It's a name that feels almost melodic. It has a rhythm, like the very thing it describes: the primal, unbroken correspondence between the body and the mind. This conversation is always happening; a constant, wordless exchange that shapes every moment of our existence. The body and mind are like those two old friends who can't help but fall into deep dialogue every time they meet. They are inseparable allies, and their relationship is not just helpful – it is fundamental to this journey towards the place that has never been wounded. Yet, somehow, amidst the clamour of modern life, we've forgotten how to listen. Culture has handed us gadgets that claim to know us better than we know ourselves: watches that measure our fitness, phones that chart our sleep cycles, and external monitors that reduce the richness of our internal experience to mere data points, graphs and metrics. And so, those two old friends, the body and the mind, stop talking. Or perhaps they still speak, but we've learned to tune them out, distracted by the static of our side-world.

This is where the credence frequency comes in. It's the name for that instinctive signal, that internal transmission we've all but abandoned. Reconnecting to it is not just important, it's essential: when the mind spins out of control and tangles itself in loops of thought, the body pulls us back.

You can't *think* your way out of a spiral. On its own, the mind can't untangle the knots it creates. Expecting the mechanisms that got you into the mess to get you out of it is like asking a dog with the zoomies to sit down: it's pointless. But the body, your steady and grounded ally, can calm the chaos. Rebuilding that connection, strengthening what I call the credence frequency – a clear, unwavering signal of truth within you – is where you learn to trust that internal instinct again.

Practices like body-scan meditations help you tune back into this connection. They teach you to anchor yourself in the body's sensations, noticing the rhythm of your breath, fully inhabiting the present moment with the body. The body becomes your tether when the world feels overwhelming or your mind races. It doesn't argue, judge or overthink. It simply is. When you learn to listen to it, you'll find a steadying resonance, a frequency that holds you, grounds you and moves you forward.

This is the credence frequency: an innate dialogue that was never truly lost, only forgotten. It's time to remember it. It's time to tune back in to it.

5. *Grace*

Our final Polaris principle of Act 1 is *grace*. Of all the principles, this is the one people often find hardest to embrace. It's strange how easily we offer compassion to others – strangers, or celebrities – yet how fiercely we withhold it from ourselves. I've seen it countless times in my work and lived it myself. For years, my inner voice was a relentless critic. It wasn't just self-doubt; it was self-sabotage disguised as protection. I told myself that if I tore myself down first, no one else could beat me to it. But add that to a cultural backdrop that encourages constant comparison – where we measure ourselves against the carefully composed highlight reels of other people's lives on social media – and it's no wonder many of us are brutal towards ourselves.

Some people overcompensate with outward displays of confidence, a bright façade to hide the cracks within; others, like me, turn inwards, using our minds as a punching bag. And I get it – offering yourself grace is hard. Even the word 'grace' might feel soft and unconvincing, like a hymn you were forced to sing in class back in primary school But grace isn't fluffy. It's a resolute, steady and spiritual strength. It's not about letting yourself off the hook or excusing everything you've done. It's about releasing the impossible expectations you carry. It's about seeing the cracks – not as failures, but as the shared, messy beauty of being human. When you move inwards, into the stillness of mindfulness, that harsh voice might get louder. Without distractions, it can feel like it's shouting through a megaphone. For me, it screamed: 'You're a fucking waster, Niall!' It was an amplified, unfiltered self-loathing. Instead of meeting that voice with anger or resistance, I began to meet it with grace. With clemency. With compassion. Think about it. You're here, taking the time to turn inwards, to face yourself honestly. That's courage, and so many never muster it. You're doing the work. You're stepping into the discomfort. That, in itself, is a rebellious act of strength and beauty. Yes, it will be brutally hard at times. But when the struggle arises, meet it – not with more struggle, but with grace.

This principle will walk beside you every step of the way, reminding you that you are not broken. You are human. And in that humanity lies a connection to everyone on this journey Together, we'll navigate towards that untainted, unbroken place within.

All that's left for me to say is this: I respect you deeply. I wish you courage, strength, and every bit of grace you can offer yourself. You're not alone. Let's take this journey together.

Chapter 1

Non-Judgement

It was a 90-minute drive from my apartment in Donnybrook in south Dublin to Tullow, a regional town in the county of Carlow in the Midlands of Ireland.

The last time I had been in Tullow, fortune had conspired against me as I got knocked out. I was playing rugby for my hometown of Mullingar under-18s when I came out second-best against an 18-stone farmer's hip. Apparently I started meowing like a cat and telling my half-bald coach that he had nice hair while simultaneously trying to punch him as he tried to guide me off the pitch. My first and, indeed, not last dance with a concussion. *Life holds a penchant for irony*, I thought. *Driving back here all those years later, trying to fix my head.*

Holding on to the last gasp of an Indian summer, you could still sense the incoming change of seasons. Almost without fail Ireland tends to get a beautiful week's weather when the kids go back to school. The kids get served two months of rain, wind and humidity with the odd flickers of sun, only to sit in the classroom for the first week back, staring out the window at Santa Ponsa. I always felt it was nature's way of compensating the parents after a summer of chaos and carnage, entertaining their kids while trying to work.

The air conditioning in the car was acting up, and there was a two-month-old protein shake that had fermented under my car seat in the heat, so the drive down involved me having my head out the window like an exuberant puppy on the way to the park. The M9 motorway to that part of the world is relatively uneventful, and with each mile I travelled from the mayhem of the city I could usually sense my central nervous system dialling down, almost unaware the anarchy and banality of everyday life had hijacked it.

That day, however, it was quite the opposite for me. A distinct discomfort rallied through my body. I was unsure whether my steady stream of sweat was due to the car's sauna-like conditions or my finely tuned and overworked evolutionary design that was preparing for battle. Either way, a light grey T-shirt was not the wisest fashion choice I had ever made.

I pulled into a lay-by about forty kilometres from Tullow. Two couples were sharing a cigarette outside their car – they may have been tourists wondering when they would get the brutal Irish weather they had been promised. I was having a 'moment', so they left me alone. These moments often feel like a catch-up scene at the start of a TV show – years of your life edited into the brevity of a single flashing memory, while your mind tends only to show you the shit scenes. The emotional charge accompanying these moments in the past would be enough to spiral me out of control.

Now, I sat on the verge of the freshly cut grass and thought, *What am I doing?*

Several months previously, I had returned to a place I had run from for many years: the arts block in University College Dublin – somewhere that would make Eastern Bloc architecture look like Claridge's. I was there to undertake an interview in the school of psychology for a place on the master's degree in mindfulness-based interventions.

I had first entered this building as a scholarship student on my first day of college nearly twenty years ago. As mentioned previously, after a panic attack, I spent most of my first day in the toilets. The following four years were a master class in avoidance and adversity. Once I got out, I promised myself I would never return, yet there I was.

But this time, it felt different, sitting in my interview with Dr Paul D'Alton and the head of the school, Louise McHugh. Paul always reminds me of Anthony Hopkins: not in a 'going to eat your brains' kind of way, but in a way where he has used his life experience and knowledge to help guide others. He does this thing with his eyebrow when he asks you a question that makes you feel like he has just gone for a guided tour of your consciousness. *God help him if he's gone in there*, I thought.

At this point, I had been practising mindfulness for several years, but this was a more profound step into the learning. I was concerned it could affect my meditation practice, but was also excited about how it could nourish and deepen it. It's important to highlight that mindfulness meditation is a skill, and like every skill, it can be developed with practice.

The interview went well, but something Paul said stayed with me as I nervously navigated my way back along the depressing corridors of the arts block: 'The master's course will commence with a five-day silent retreat.'

For me, at that time, silence felt less like peace and more like being mugged by my thoughts. I managed it in my mindfulness practice, for I was only an eye-open away from the noise and distraction of the external world, but this would be a different challenge. All my life, I'd embraced chaos and surrounded myself with the din of discordance. I was comfortable with it. I was on a constant quest for cacophony. Silence made way for thinking, and I didn't need any help with that, thank you very much.

Although I had spent many years in therapy, I was still stuck in a state of aversion and avoidance. I had come so far in many ways, but there were ever-present life traps I constantly found myself stuck in. I became pathologically obsessive about certain aspects of my life. In particular, exercise, work and success. And because these were 'healthy' behaviours, I never recognised them for what they were: smokescreens. I believed my happiness lay in achievement. I had become so busy chasing a life, that I ultimately was missing *living* a life.

But something happens in the frequency of silence, where you have no choice but to face the parts of yourself that you would prefer not to see. There's nowhere to run when your thoughts are doing the mugging.

I returned to the car and waved goodbye to the slightly concerned-looking tourists half-lost in a haze of cigarette smoke.

Teach Bhride Convent in Tullow was a 25-minute drive from the lay-by, and was my home for the next five days. Pulling into the car park, I got that wave of breath-robbing dread that always tends to accompany me to any place that reminds me of primary school. The shadow of the local church spire spread out across the lawn as the warm, setting sun fell behind the horizon. My education in the hands of the Christian Brothers meant that any faith I had had was quite literally beaten out of me. It took me a long time to separate the power and peace of faith and spirituality from the insidious nature of institutional religion. I had also wasted my time over the years watching too many low-budget horror movies, so I automatically accepted that the convent was no doubt haunted and I would wake in the middle of the night with a nun conjured at the end of my bed giving me the side-eye for my years of Catholic neglect. And, of course, I wouldn't be able to scream for help because it was a silent retreat.

I think, therefore I catastrophise. Descartes would be proud. Or worried.

Walking up to the front doors, a memory of my mother dropping me off on my first day of school at the Presentation Convent Junior Infants in Mullingar surged through my mind. These places all looked the same: allergic to a coat of paint, and massive windows you could see out of but not in through.

My family had taken bets on how long I would last in silence till I lost my mind. You would not have got odds at Paddy Power of me lasting. But while I may have had a visceral fear of silence, they also underestimated my granite-like stubbornness, especially when a few quid was on the line. Walking through the Gothically creaking wooden doors, my new classmates, and my teachers, Helen and Jo, greeted me. There was a welcoming softness in their eyes – or a pity. It was hard to tell the difference.

I was handed my room key; I was on the top floor, hopefully well away from any nuns of the supernatural variety. The stairs creaked and moaned; I half expected them to fall in as I thumped up them like a teenager in a huff. Once there, I groaned – the bed looked like it would have a tough time catering for a six foot six chap like myself. Actually, I didn't think I would have fit in it when I was five, but I thought it best not to ask for another room on my first day. We had been asked not to bring books or phones. All I had was a half empty bag, one change of clothes, and a picnic of service station snacks. *I might not be able to talk, but I will surely eat.* Dinner was served at 7 p.m., and then our teachers delivered a short induction on what to expect over the coming five days. After that, we went to bed, and upon waking, we would be in silence, apart from the guidance of our teachers.

Getting into my infant-sized bed, I had some adult-sized thoughts. Any chance I had of finding some sleep was totalled by the fact my room was beside the communal toilets, whose plumbing system had not been updated since the Irish Famine. Sure enough, sleep eluded me.

I arrived at breakfast powered by regret and the promise of toast. A number of my classmates were already sitting reverently at the tables. There was no eye contact. The only sounds were cutlery clashing off plates and the uniquely irritating noise of human chewing. I burnt my tongue on the piping-hot porridge. It was a good thing I would not need it for the next five days.

After breakfast, we had our first practice in the communal area. Each place was set up within a circle. I sat on the ground as Jo brought us through a guided practice. I noticed that there was a specific type of chaos occupying my mind. I was caught between the rumination of shame and self-reproach and the fear of a future where I would not be able to shake it off. With that, I started to use myself as a punching bag. I made myself the villain, the fool and the fraud all in one breath. What was I even doing there? There was a viciousness to this internal appraisal. There was an intensity to this inner voice. Like the drill sergeant scene in Stanley Kubrick's *Full Metal Jacket*.

An hour in, I was ready to walk straight out the door and drive back to Dublin. Who in my family would win the money? Instead, I took a walk outside in the convent garden. There was something in me that was convincing me to stay. A voice that was trying to speak over the drill sergeant's barrelling roars.

The next few days were like a fever dream. I lost time and space between sleep and social deprivation – life at 0.25x speed. There was a crooked anger in me that I had not felt before – grief in unfamiliar clothing, that I was now being forced to wear in this frequency of silence. We would sit for hours each day, meditating, while I attempted to confront this unrelenting force. I often opened my eyes, looked around the room, and wondered if I was the only one trapped in this darkness.

The truth is, I doubt I was.

I was navigating a pounding cluster headache on the morning of the fourth day. At this point, I was sleeping on the floor as the bed springs had decided they had had enough. I could sense the finish line, but it still felt miles away. At breakfast that morning, I knocked my coffee off the table, which was the most exciting thing that had happened in days.

I made my way up to the communal area for practice. There was an energy of vulnerability in the room. I always felt that vulnerability was the alliance of delicacy and power. A sweet spot where the soul opens itself to the world and is not afraid of what the world observes. As the guided practice commenced, Helen encouraged us to consider the attitudes of a good friend. What do we value in a friend or someone we love? Friends and family flashed into my mind. I thought of the compassion, empathy, forgiveness, loyalty and honesty they unconditionally offered me – those moments in my life when they held me in my fear. They were the emotional scaffolding holding me up when I felt like I couldn't stand alone, a light in the darkness.

I thought of my parents' clemency when I fucked up as a teenager. My teammates' support after a loss. I even thought of the limitless love dogs have offered me. What had pressed against my chest for days began to ease, losing its shape, its urgency. The drill sergeant's voice softened. Then I thought of how all these people in my life, no matter how destructive or chaotic my behaviours had been over the years, had never judged me, no matter how hurtful or dismissive I may have been.

And with this, I fell apart. The realisation that the virtues you value in a good friend are not virtues you offer to yourself can hit hard. I was trying to disguise my muted sobs with deep breaths, but I was fooling nobody. But I wasn't ashamed or embarrassed.

I was released.

My good friend and mentor, Dr Tony Bates, once spoke of a woman he had treated, telling me that she said she was 'always looking for stop-and-go signs in other people's eyes'. That was me. I constantly sought validation from others because I didn't trust myself – but this habit hid a deeper, more destructive pattern. By pre-emptively judging myself harshly, I believed I could 'beat others to the punch'. If I criticised myself first, their disapproval would lose its power over me. It was a twisted form of protection: self-abuse as a shield against external rejection. Yet in reality, I was only reinforcing my own insecurity, sabotaging relationships, careers and dreams in the process.

That was why the concept of non-judgement was so raw. And why that moment of realisation in Tullow was overwhelming, yet utterly transformative.

My entire life revolved around judgement: professionally, socially and personally. As a professional athlete, I was hardwired to judge. Every detail of performance and ability was forensically monitored. My body became an implement of work and exploitation. I outsourced it. The body frayed like overworked ropes, until one day the rope inevitability snapped. Until that point in life, my identity had been wrapped around being an athlete first.

Moving from professional sports to music was out of the frying pan into the fire. Only then, it wasn't my body being judged; it was my creative output. When your entire self-worth gets submerged in the success of your creative output, it gets very messy. My every profession from then on had involved nuclear-level scrutiny and judgement, making it a default setting that I applied to every aspect of my life.

This paradox haunted my practice. I would sit to meditate and spend most of it directing abuse at myself. 'You are shit at this,' and 'Why are you even trying?' or 'You are wasting your time.' I had become so used to judgement that I was unaware I was doing this within my practice. I was desensitised to it. But I began to realise that there was enough judgement in my life.

NON-JUDGEMENT

I wanted to make this space, this internal world, this frequency of silence, a place where judgement was unnecessary.

Let me bring you back to that voice convincing me to stay as I walked around the convent's grounds. Meister Eckhart, the mystic and philosopher from the 13th century, once offered a quote that has stayed with me from the first moment I read it: 'There is a place in the soul where you have never been wounded.' Eckhart saw the divine not as distant or separate but as something intimately woven into the very fabric of our being. His words remind us that no matter how life bruises or breaks us, there's a part of us, a sacred, unshakable core, that remains untouched: the spirit. This place exists beyond pain, beyond failure, beyond loss. It's not something we need to build or earn; it's already there, waiting for us to rediscover it.

When the world feels intense or adrift, I return to Eckhart's words. They remind me that healing isn't about repairing what's shattered; it's about reconnecting with that inner place where we are still fully ourselves.

This was the place communicating with me that day. It exists within every one of us, but many of us cannot hear it. The chaos and noise of our external worlds drown it out, and our drill sergeant screams over every message it sends.

The modern world has also weaponised the use of judgement and, at times, it can feel like the Hunger Games. So, all of a sudden, this straightforward definition seems to grate against how we live our lives. Just because you close your eyes, burn some incense and listen to whale music doesn't mean all this noise mutes itself. Quite the opposite: it can often feel like your thoughts are amplified through a massive PA system as you stand beside the speaker. And with these thoughts often come feelings and sensations, and before you know it, you are so far from the present moment, and throwing shade at yourself for being so pathetically unskilled at meditation.

Let me paint a picture . . .

You sit down at the end of a long day to start a practice. You shut your eyes and begin by focusing on the movement of the breath. A thought enters the mind: *I forgot to ring Emma. Oh god, Emma already doesn't like me. It is going to be so awkward the next time I see her. Will I get a pizza later? There are over 1500 calories in a pizza, and I'm eating so much shit lately. Will I go to the gym before or after work tomorrow? Work isn't going well. I need to leave my job, but I'm hitting my thirties now and need to settle down. I'm so useless at this meditation nonsense. I knew I would be. It's a waste of time. My head is just too messed up, I'm just too messed up . . . Fuck it, I'll just open one eye and check my phone . . .* Now, you're down a rabbit hole. What started as a single thought became an entire discourse and narrative, a Christopher Nolan film. You went down the rabbit hole and did not come back. And while you were down there, you also decided to tear into yourself. You ended up even more rinsed, anxious and frazzled than when you started.

That can no doubt demotivate and disincentivise anyone who wants to continue practising mindfulness and find that place within themselves that has never been wounded. But let me reshape the above experience . . .

You sit down at the end of a long day to start a practice. You shut your eyes and begin by focusing on the movement of the breath. A thought enters the mind: *I forgot to ring Emma . . . Back to the breath – there's no need for judgement for being distracted: the mind is only doing what the mind likes to do. It's only doing its job and going on a bit of a wander. Will I get a pizza later? . . . Back to the breath. The mind seems dynamic this evening, but that's okay. Return to the present moment by focusing on the breath . . . And so on.*

NON-JUDGEMENT

No judgement, no beating yourself up for your wondering mind . . . just acceptance and move on.

A Buddhist monk, Shunryū Suzuki, said: 'Leave your front and back doors open. Let thoughts come and go. Just don't serve them tea.' The idea of stopping thoughts is a myth. We are not trying to do that in meditation. We observe them and let them walk through our heads without offering them a cup of tea and Bourbon creams before shouting a tirade of abuse at them.

So, as we start this journey, we become aware of this judgemental mind. Notice it, tip your hat to it. But see what it feels like to let go of the need to judge your experience: the surround-sound judgement that is such a trait of our modern world does not serve us in our practice. Becoming aware of it is our first Polaris principle and the initial step towards the place that has never been wounded.

Audio track

The opening notes of Chapter 1's soundtrack are as unassuming as a single breath: a simple composition that creates a vast, unspoken space for the listener. It isn't just music; it's a practice, an invitation to pause and witness. To observe the gentle rise and fall of the breath, untainted by judgement and detached from expectation. Its simplicity is its power.

I remember the first time my fingers played these chords, forming as if they'd been waiting for me all along. A piece of music that acknowledged the truths at the beginning of any journey: the anxieties that creep in, the unease of the unknown. But also, just beneath that, excitement and curiosity; that unnameable spark of possibility that invites you forward, even when your feet are hesitant to follow, just like it happened for me as I walked up to those convent doors in Tullow.

The piece needed to encompass all of that. It needed to meet the listener where they were at, whether in doubt or hope, and offer a kind of shelter. It did not erase those feelings but observed them, and allowed them to exist without the need to judge.

As I played, I could feel the music becoming that shelter, a warm, welcoming space to land, a place where everything could coexist: the worry, the wonder, the fear, the hope; a space wide enough to contain all of it.

Chapter 2

Untethering

Carrying the heavy burden of the past can make you weary. And more often than not, it's not your weight to carry.

A dark history doesn't have to shadow the future; mistakes gone before can be our best teacher, but we must learn, honour that legacy, so we never return.

The unease of facing a road unknown can alone paralyse the pendulum.

Reflections and memoirs of the mind, loss in time, aspirations, a design for life, so busy chasing that we miss the living, so busy doing that we forget the being.

Thoughts will cross your path, and emotions will hijack the way, entice you off route, and lead you astray.

But the place that's never been wounded remains unchanged, standing timeless, ready to receive us.

That brings us to our second Polaris principle of the untethering, the letting go.

We can attach our experience to that which brings us joy, peace, and pleasure.

Grasp tightly to the solace of feeling at ease, enough.

Or we can retreat from the pain of a lost love, adverse to the suffering that will at times come up.

We want to run away, not towards, numb and avoid, but we remain on this path of presence, letting go of the need to have any other experience than the one we have in each moment, each breath, each step.

THE PLACE THAT HAS NEVER BEEN WOUNDED

We embrace impermanence and the fleeting flow of feelings.
We let them go their own way.
Untethered from allowing thoughts, emotions and feelings to dictate the course, we know the direction in which we must stay.

It was a question I never expected to be asked. My reply was clumsy, awkward, evasive, a fumbling attempt to sidestep the crushing truth that the person asking it was living on borrowed time. Her request was one I couldn't refuse, yet I felt compelled to offer some hollow reassurance, to suggest that maybe, just maybe, she'd survive this. Perhaps I'd never have to fulfil her wish; the doctors were wrong, and we'd all skip off into some sunset together.

Vicky's smile was faint, almost automatic, as if my attempt at vague optimism had triggered a polite but well-worn reaction. But her eyes told a different story. They had a weary understanding, as though she'd witnessed this kind of maladroit evasion a hundred times before. She appeared accustomed to how people skirted the truth as if shielding her – or perhaps themselves – from its weight. Her silence screamed, echoing all the words I had not managed to say, and at that moment, I was starkly confronted by my inadequacies.

'When the time comes, I want you to sing "Postcards" at my funeral.'

'Postcards' is a song that I wrote for friends who lost a young child. They were left without the closure of a final goodbye. I wanted to write words that acted as a postcard sent from their son to them. It was the only way I knew to offer comfort during a time of such harrowing loss. The song became a consoling anthem for those struggling through grief's dark and lonely halls, becoming a bridge between what was said and all that never got to be said. Grief is the weight of those unfinished conversations, the love that never found its voice.

I took the request as one of the greatest honours of my life, though it was mixed with the restless realisation that Vicky would not be there when I played it for her. Also, I had doubts lingering: something I couldn't push away. Years earlier, I'd been asked to play at the funeral of someone I cared about deeply. I didn't get far. A few chords in, my hands started to shake, and my voice broke. The weight of the moment fractured me. I stood at the altar with a voice I wasn't sure would hold, offering a song to someone I'd never stop carrying. It was a courage I had not prepared for.

It wasn't sadness as such, but a closeness, and almost an awkwardness, trying to offer something when everything felt like it was falling apart. That kind of vulnerability is not something you can rehearse for. And yet, here I was, two decades into a career that had taken me to some of the biggest stages in the world, still wrestling with that same dread. But performing for thousands is one thing – it's loud, chaotic and a shared energy that carries you through – while singing for one person or for a room full of grieving folks, holding their breath, waiting for the music to say what words cannot: that's something else entirely. I've learned a lot over the years: how can you hold a crowd, silence a room, and turn a song into something that freezes time. But this was different. This wasn't about performance. It was about presence and saluting their memory, simply showing up, even when you just want to run. But I could not run from this.

We sat outside a pub on Kilkee's main street, two crusading compadres clinging to the last dregs of a midsummer evening. The sun was doing its best as a reluctant houseguest, hanging around just long enough to be polite before falling off behind the cliffs. The shade was creeping in, all chilly and smug, but we weren't moving. Not yet. Kilkee, a little seaside village in County Clare, had that effect; it made us want to stay put, even when our fingers started to numb.

The Atlantic, for once, wasn't throwing a tantrum. After a week of unseasonal high pressure, the ocean had finally decided to behave itself. It lay there, all calm and glinting, like it hadn't spent the last seven days trying to carve apart the already time-worn headland. But you could still hear the low rumble of the tide and the way it whispered to the sand, like they were sharing gossip. And then, cutting through the spacing of each wave, the shrieks of kids who'd forgotten how cold Irish seawater could be. They were splashing about, laughing like they'd discovered some salty secret, while the rest of us sat there, wrapped in jumpers, wondering if we'd ever been that brave.

The pub behind us was doing its thing, glasses clinking, voices rising and falling, someone murdering an Irish ballad in the corner after 14 stouts and even more missed calls from a pissed-off partner. But out here, it was just us, the fading light and the kind of peace that makes you forget, for a second, that life is mostly chaos but also precious in these fleeting moments. The type of peace that makes you want to stay forever.

But I had a show to play. Just up the road, me and the lads from The Blizzards were set to headline a festival that night. I'd come down early to meet a few friends and soak up the kind of hospitality that only this part of the country seems to offer: warm, unpretentious and laced with just enough hedonism to keep things interesting. The setlist had already been decided, and it included 'Postcards'. After the conversation I'd just had, I was unsure I would get through it without my voice cracking or my brain short-circuiting.

I turned to Vicky, who was heading to the gig later with a gang of friends, and asked her straight: 'Would it be okay if I played it?' Her reply was everything I needed to know about her personality's sheer, unvarnished brilliance. She didn't miss a beat. 'Jesus Christ, Niall,' she said, deadpan, as she put down her drink, 'I'm not ready to die yet, but of course, I'd love you to play it.'

Laughing so hard I nearly toppled off the stool, I spat the cheap merlot I was drinking all over myself. That was the thing about Vicky; she had this way of cutting through the heaviness with a line so sharp and perfectly timed that she could have given Billy Connolly a run for his money. I told her we would meet them after the show and made my way to the venue, still weak from laughing at her whip-smart wit.

Describing Vicky Phelan isn't easy, and maybe that's because she was the kind of person who defied the very notion of being captured by language. She was a force, a presence, a light that seemed to burn brighter the darker the world around her became. Our paths first crossed because of our shared work in social advocacy, though to say it was 'work' feels too small and too clinical. It was more than that; it was a calling, a shared understanding that life is not just about surviving but also about fighting for something greater than ourselves. We would seek each other out at events and awards. Vicky had an almost pathological inability to tolerate bullshit. It was like observing a great artist at work, calling out the foghorns of nonsense you would often have to endure at such events. But Vicky could still do it with measured diplomacy, a firm kindness and frankness that could take the varnish off an old chair. This alchemy of traits, of nuclear-powered courage and tenacity, collided to shape one of the most important voices in Irish history.

And hers was a voice that didn't just stand for something; it stood against everything that tried to silence it. And that, more than anything, was what made her unforgettable. She was not just a woman of her time but a force for all time. Power thrives in silence, but it crumbles before the brave. Whistleblowers and truth-tellers are the ones who stand in the storm, unflinching. Vicky is the most fearless person I have ever known. She spoke her truth, even as the world tried to silence her. In her courage, she became a mirror, reflecting both the ugliness of power and the strength it takes to defy it.

In 2014, Vicky was diagnosed with cervical cancer. In an audit carried out that year, it was established that, three years earlier, in 2011, a smear test reported as clear was found to be incorrect. However, this information was never passed on to her, due to an error in the system. This failure was part of a broader issue with the national screening programme, where similar mistakes had gone unnoticed, and many women were, therefore, uninformed of the risks they faced.

Vicky brought a groundbreaking legal action against the Irish Health Service Executive and the US laboratory that had wrongly interpreted her smear test. In 2018, she accepted a settlement, but she got one message across: she would not be muted. Vicky turned down the confidentiality agreement and revealed the truth to the public, bringing to light a scandal that remains one of the greatest shames in Irish medical history. It was only because of her decision that hundreds of other women who were potentially affected could finally know the truth about their missed diagnoses: over 220 women in Ireland had been affected by the same catastrophic failures. Smear tests had been misread, warning signs missed, yet many of these women were never told; left in the dark about results from audits that could have saved their lives. It wasn't just a system failure; it was a failure to protect the people the programme was meant to safeguard. A failure of trust.

Vicky was a fearless voice for women's health, demanding changes in a system that had failed so many. She fought for patient rights, truth and real accountability in medical care.

In 2018, she received the news no one should have to hear: her cancer was terminal. But she refused to surrender. She refused to stay silent, using the time she had left to push for change, aware that while it was too late for her, others still had a chance. She also fought for access to a groundbreaking immunotherapy treatment used in the US, an option not initially available in Ireland. Her determination gave her a chance at more time and paved the way for other women to access similar life-saving treatments.

On 14 November, 2022, I received the call that Vicky's courageous fight for survival had ended. Her pain was finally over. I put new strings on my guitar, polished it up, sat in my sitting room and played 'Postcards'. A few days later, I sat by the altar in the Church of the Assumption in Mooncoin, County Kilkenny, Vicky's place of birth, and I honoured her wish.

'*I am still here, I am the light that's surrounding you every time your darkness comes.*'

Driving back after the funeral, in the silence of my thoughts, I recalled my conversation with Vicky that night, after our show. The pub we'd been in threatened a lock-in: a consensual kidnapping where the doors shut, time vanishes, and poor decisions feel like triumphs. By dawn, you're deep in a debate about 1990s boy bands with a stranger holding up the bar. The fallout? A four- to five-day convalescence, especially brutal when you're nudging your forties and existential dread is part of your daily routine. Yet, you wear it like a badge of honour because, in Ireland, surviving a lock-in isn't just a night out; it's a story you'll half remember and wildly exaggerate.

That night, we barely touched a drop. We were too lost in conversation to be distracted by the need to lift a glass and interrupt the flow of the discussion. The chaos around us blurred into nothing – drunken shite-talk, tone-deaf renditions of 'The Whole of the Moon' belted out by some lad still in Bermuda shorts and a fast-food-stained T-shirt, the clatter of glasses and the hum of the pub – it all faded like static. Because when Vicky spoke, her voice cut through it all. Clear, steady, present. It was as if she was trying to pour something into me, some wisdom she'd carved out of her own life, in the mirror of her mortality. She saw things so sharply through that lens, and she wanted me to see them, too. It was not a sermon, but came out of this fierce, unshakable hope that maybe I could carry a piece of it forward.

Vicky had a way of disarming those in her presence. The more I got to know her, the more comfortable I felt engaging in more profound, philosophical discourse. There was nothing I cherished more than simply listening to her. It wasn't just about hearing her words; it was about being fully present and letting her voice weave through the silence between us while I held back my own. She found comfort in it, too, in being heard without interruption, without judgement.

And if you can manage to shut me up for over a few moments, you must have some presence.

I asked her, as sensitively as possible, 'How do you bear it all? How do you move through the world, carrying what you do, and still find the strength to go on?'

The question hung there, suspended, as if the room held its breath, waiting for her reply. I was also conscious of not hijacking her night by asking such questions. But in moments like this, you tap into your intuition. It felt like I was invited, not crashing the party.

Vicky paused – knowing her wicked sense of humour, it was as much to make me drown in an awkward silence as it was to prepare a response. She finally put me out of my mortified misery. 'Niall, I had to learn to let go. I don't know how much time I have left with my children, and I want to be fully present for them, not trapped in the past, reliving what was done to me. Those things I can't change, I can no longer control. But I can choose how I show up for them now, and the memories I want them to hold on to when I am gone.'

I've always felt a compulsion to fill the quiet after something profound is said with words that feel safe, almost automatic. A soft 'So true,' or a murmured 'Amazing,' tossed out like a lifebuoy; not for them, but for me. It's never dismissive, not really. It's more like a reflex, a way to buy myself a second to breathe, to process the weight of what's just been laid bare. But at that moment, any words I could have mustered would have felt hollow, like trying to hold an ocean in a thimble. Silence wasn't just easier; it was the only thing that made sense.

After a moment, I asked her, 'What about the *anger?*'

'It's still there. And so is the fear,' she replied in a hushed voice, almost as if she were saying it to herself now.

Her righteous anger has changed Ireland forever, and I will hold on to the conversation we shared that warm summer night in County Clare forever, too.

Our life experiences and the lessons we gather come from countless directions, like rivers charting their paths through the landscape of who we are. Some find wisdom in the pages of books; others in the words of peers, teachers or the guidance of role models. Some learn by living, falling and rising, by the unfiltered madness of experience. For me, the most significant truths have always emerged in moments like this – shared conversations where hearts and minds meet in a space of vulnerability and humanity. Wisdom is offered in countless ways, but it's only when we open ourselves to it and let it seep into the cracks of ourselves that it truly leaves its mark.

THE PLACE THAT HAS NEVER BEEN WOUNDED

Throughout my mindfulness journey, there have been elements of the work that have challenged me immensely. When I would sit in my presence, my mind would replay, ruminate and retaliate with memories and emotional charges that made it almost impossible to remain aware. The vividness of some of my past memories was often terrifying. A moment would rise, shattering the stillness and inviting the all-too-familiar wave of panic to flood in. I kept trying to control it, to steer the experience, to dictate where my mind should go during meditation, much like I tried to control everything else in my life. I clung to an idea of how the practice 'should' feel, how I 'should' be. But mindfulness does not work like that. It's not about bending the moment to your will; it's about letting it bend you, and having the psychological flexibility to move through it.

At first, it can feel disorientating to detach from controlling our experience. Much of our anxiety is driven by the absence of control, and it's only natural to try and manipulate our practice so it will be pleasant, comforting or enriching. And at times, it may well be. But at other times, it will be suffocating and paralysing. This is the practice – the *untethering* from the need to design your meditation, which can be both liberating and unnerving. It can feel like being caught in a riptide. Your instinct is to swim against it, but the best action is to let go. At first, it feels like surrender, an admission that you are not the architect of this moment. But slowly, almost imperceptibly, it becomes something else: an invitation to stop trying so hard, to stop forcing the experience into a shape it was never meant to hold, to liberate yourself from the need to regulate thoughts, feelings and emotions and observe what is there. And in that space, where effort falls away, something richer emerges – not the meditation you imagined, but the one you needed.

We all carry a past that can both haunt and nourish us, a vast spectrum of experiences that shape who we are. We all face a future that fills us with equal parts dread and hope, a horizon we can't quite see but can't stop imagining. Both are largely beyond our grasp, echoes of what was and whispers of what might be. But here, in the present moment, we have something rare: agency. A chance to breathe, to choose, to be. But this choice to be present, to untangle ourselves from the past or the unscripted tomorrow, isn't just for meditation. It's there for us in the mess and beauty of our everyday lives. With the people we love in our personal, social and professional worlds, even as modern culture bombards us with videos and posts urging us to chase the life we want rather than embracing the one right in front of us. So much of my own life has been spent in the shadowed spaces of regret, shame and worry, but through the steadying wisdom of awareness, I've learned to strive for presence, to anchor myself in the moment. It doesn't always work. Some days, the pull of old habits or future fears is too strong. But over time, you begin to loosen your grip on fleeting desires, heavy burdens and the need to control what's already gone or yet to come. In the words of Jack Kornfield, 'Letting go is the path to freedom.'[2]

And as we continue on this path towards the untainted, unaffected steady and consistent part of ourselves, we trust that we know the way. There will be things that meet us on this journey. Distractions, doubts and fears will rise like shadows, whispering promises of short cuts or warnings of dead ends. They will try to pull us off course and make us question the steps we have taken and the ones we have yet to take. But here is the thing: we don't have to fight them. We don't have to wrestle them into submission. We just have to let go. Let go of the need to control, to predict, to perfect. Let go of the idea that we should have it all figured out.

THE PLACE THAT HAS NEVER BEEN WOUNDED

We untether. We release the grip on the reins, the need to dictate every turn, every stumble, every rise and fall. We don't need to know what's around the next bend. We need to stay present with each step. Each breath, without judgement.

I find myself thinking about Vicky a lot. The modern world has a way of rushing forward, of brushing past the things that should never be forgotten. But I will never forget Vicky. Not her. Not what she taught me. Nor her bravery, her courage; her fierce, unrelenting determination to do the right thing in a world that often feels like it's lost its moral compass. Vicky was one of those rare souls who reminds us, who reminded me, that at the core of us all, beneath the noise and the upheaval and the fear, there is a part of ourselves that knows what's right. That part that refuses to bend, even when the world's weight tries to break it. She lived from that place, unapologetically, unflinchingly. And in doing so, she showed the rest of us how to do the same. We owe her so much. Not just for what she did but for who she was. For the light she carried, even when the world around her felt impossibly dark. Because that is the thing about people like Vicky: they remind us that there are lights in this world that can never be put out. Their light endures no matter how heavy the darkness or deep the shadows. And in that there is hope. There is always hope.

Audio track

The piece I composed for this chapter is one of the more deeply felt piano motifs I've composed. It's not a meditation designed to still the mind or lull the soul into quiet. It's a reflection that is almost restless in its honesty. It's a short, spoken-word fragment, a fleeting moment of clarity

UNTETHERING

that tries to capture the dynamic essence of untethering, that act of letting go, of releasing something you've held on to for too long, even if it hurts to open your hand.

When the piano melody begins to flow, it's meant to mirror that sensation of surrender, like watching a feather caught in the wind, carried away without resistance. There's a beauty in that release.

It's a piece about loss and the strange, almost sacred freedom that comes when you stop holding on so tightly. When you let the wind take you where it will.

I wrote it for Vicky in her memory, and sometimes, when I play it, I swear I can feel her presence beside me.

Chapter 3

The Novice Soul

'We are calling on the Irish Government and Irish government authorities to honour the memory of 1,304 deceased Irish citizens in a mass grave on the grounds of St Loman's Hospital, Mullingar.'

The Uplift petition lingered at the top of my inbox, unopened; in the past, the words *St Loman's* alone could rob me of breath and paralyse any semblance of rationale and logic.

Opened in 1855 under the grim and unyielding title of 'The Mullingar District Lunatic Asylum', its obsidian-dark walls and imposing Victorian silhouette have haunted the Mullingar skyline for generations. It cast a shadow that felt inescapable, as though it moved with you, stretching just far enough to remind you of its presence. Walking past, you couldn't shake the eerie sensation that, at any moment, it might extend unseen arms and draw you into its depths. As a child, I had a recurring nightmare of being dragged inside the door of the towering red chimney furnace around the back of the hospital as my parents desperately attempted to reach my outstretched hands. As a troubled adolescent, I carried an unrelenting dread that if I ever spoke of the carnage that reigned within me, I too would be committed to St Loman's, alongside the lost souls that shuffled around the grounds of the hospital, long having let go of the hope that they would ever experience life in the absence of coercion and control.

As young fools, under the relentless weight of peer pressure, we hurled cruel taunts at these patients, our voices sharp, immature and venomous. The nurses, their faces masks of weary empathy, stood between us and them, arms outstretched, before snapping back at us with threats. 'Shut the fuck up, or we'll call your parents.' We were products of our conditioning, ignorant and narrow-minded, driven by a fear of what we didn't understand. We had no grasp of the truth beyond our sheltered lives, no sense of the reality we mocked so thoughtlessly. I was also driven by curiosity, even at that age. What happened to these souls? How did they end up there? I found myself suspended in that strange, murky space between fear and empathy, a bewildering territory for a young lad trying to make sense of the world and his place in it.

No matter where you go, I imagine most towns and cities carry their own whispered stories about asylums and institutions: tales that dwell in the shadows, half-forgotten but never entirely gone.

The email remained unopened. Mentally, I was in a particularly fragile state, and my habitual tendency to self-sacrifice would have flattened me if I had got involved in the campaign. The latent legacy of fear and apathy was too much to face in the haze of my numbness.

Some years later, a friend tagged me in a Facebook post. 'This is a fucking disgrace.' There is nothing quite like hyperbolic sensationalism to get someone's attention. I clicked on the link, driven by a mix of naive curiosity and an overzealous urge to understand what had stirred such indignation in my drama-magnet friend. He had always been the *Dawson's Creek*-type growing up – one of those lads who found his soapbox in community forums, where he'd rant about everything from dog shit on paths to poorly lit streets and inappropriate jogging attire. I braced myself, although I wasn't expecting anything too alarming. But there it was again: St Loman's' inescapable shadow looming. The same Uplift petition I had once been too afraid to open now sat before me, commanding attention.

But this time, something had shifted. My mind, once a storm of uncertainty, was in a far stronger and more open place. So, I clicked the link. I let myself read on, knowing I should be ready for whatever it was about to stir up this time.

> 1,304 deceased patients of St Loman's Hospital, Mullingar, County Westmeath, are buried without individual grave markings – one of these is my great gran Julia Leonard (née Caffrey). My family and I discovered this after our application to have her remains exhumed to be re-interred in a family plot was turned down.
>
> Following this, I visited the graveyard and discovered [that] 1,304 men and women, including my great gran, are in what has been allowed to become a mass grave. In 2011 the HSE sanctioned graveyard maintenance work, resulting in the removal of all the crosses marking each grave. I have heard these crosses are stored in a shed on the grounds of the hospital. The last person buried here was in 1970. These deceased patients were forgotten by Irish society while interred in what was then known as the Asylum. I want to remember these people today and afford them some dignity and respect by marking their graves properly.[3]

I sensed the goosebumps rise along my neck. In front of me was a photograph of Julia Leonard with her children. And for reasons I couldn't quite explain, it felt as though I had seen it before, even though I knew I couldn't have. But something about it reached beyond the surface. It was as though the image was pulling me in in some strange, almost spiritual way, urging me to help tell her story. It's hard to put this feeling into words but at that moment, it was as if the photograph didn't just show her life; it invited me into it. She reached through the frame, asking me to see and remember her. And I couldn't look away. I surprised myself with the depth of emotion it induced. But there's always been something inside me: a hunger for meaning. I need to feel that, in some way, I am contributing to the world and not throwing stones at a problem. It's a drive that has burned in me for as long as I can remember, often to my detriment.

And then I saw a contact number on the petition for Julie Clarke, Julia's great-granddaughter. She lived in Galway, and as it so happened, I was heading there the next day with The Blizzards, to support the Black Eyed Peas. It felt like serendipity, like the universe had quietly nudged me into place. I didn't hesitate. I dialled the number.

When Julie answered, her voice was soft, but a natural warmth, rhythm and vibrato made her such a compelling communicator. It was as if she had been waiting for my call. There was an unspoken relief in her voice, a settling release, because finally, someone else was willing to help amplify this story, a story that so many had tried to silence. As I sat on a bench in Eyre Square in the middle of Galway city on a blisteringly hot summer afternoon, it felt like I was speaking with the ghost of Julia Leonard, while Vicky sat beside me on the bench.

One of the most insightful lessons my mindfulness practice gifted me was a rather unexpected one. The transition from youthful innocence to the weight of grown-up realities, complete with responsibilities and disappointments, can be more jarring than we realise and faster than we're prepared for. In the wildness of youth, discovery feels endless, and there's a romance to it. Our experiences seem limitless, and the path ahead is uncertain, but there's a vibrant comfort in not knowing what comes next. Sometimes, uncertainty is freeing; it's as if the lack of a clear direction permits us to let life unfold without the pressure of figuring it all out. But then, we pull on our metaphorical 'big boy pants', and something slips away unnoticed: the unrefined, unfiltered wonder of the world around us. We become more guarded. In all its imperfections, the world starts to chip away at that innocence, that untamed sense of awe. Somewhere along the way, we stop looking at the world with unspoiled wonder and start witnessing it through the lens of expectations, judgements and the heavy burden of experience.

When I was younger, I never had much love for video games or television; if the weather allowed – even when it didn't – I was outside, knee-deep in adventure, satisfying the curiosity of my wild imagination during days spent outside, exploring. My mother would be waiting when I eventually staggered back through the door for my potato waffles and chicken nuggets, caked in five layers of shite and dirt. It took industrial effort to scrape me clean, often involving a combination of hot water, stubbornness and the occasional threat of a squirt from the garden hose. In the truest sense, I was a child of nature, wild, curious, and utterly at home playing with worms. I operated on an ingrained instinct, a built-in framework that embraced mindfulness habitually.

In its simplest form, relearning mindfulness gave me a chance to reclaim that curiosity, to see again with the eyes of wild youth, free from the weight of cynicism or defeat. It reminded me that wonder isn't something we lose as we grow; it's something we forget how to find. It's always there, waiting to be rediscovered, if only we stop long enough to look. Naturally, as we stumble into the shaky arms of adulthood, we encounter a more profound sense of responsibility for ourselves and those surrounding us. Our intentions change, and expectations and comparisons become a daily mind riot in which we can fall between the cracks of apathy, existential dread and glory all in the same day. Adults long for the comfort of control so they can limit the anxiety and stress that come with the not-knowing we embraced so much as children.

Added to this, the cultural landscape we now find ourselves in has never been so awash with information. On the one hand, it's a limitless, infinite library for those curious to learn, but it also creates some societal entitlement to knowledge. Our curiosity can be satisfied by the few seconds it takes the satellites to beam the information back to the little box in our hand. Then we move on to the next thing that has got our attention in a headlock. The bandwidth of curiosity and cognitive focus we possess gets rinsed by the endless bullshit that blitzes our brains each day, so that the simple discoveries that used to lift our spirits are now barely even recognised. We find ourselves pulled down rabbit holes where, instead of engaging with something meaningful, we're lost in absurd online debates, like Elon Musk sparring with a teenager from Ohio over the validity of climate science. In the process, the things that used to spark wonder now struggle to compete with the mindless cacophony, leaving us numb, disoriented and far too tuned in to the wrong frequency. The truth is, this stuff is designed by people far more intelligent than I am, experts who know precisely how to hijack our attention and keep us hooked. It's a subtle game; I'm just as susceptible as anyone else. But the greatest casualty of this game has been the loss of wonder and curiosity, the very qualities that once defined my youth.

This open, unguarded way of seeing the world is what Buddhist psychology refers to as the 'beginner's mind'. Somewhere along the way, I arrived at a point where nothing seemed to surprise me any more. I fell into a kind of autopilot, where new experiences barely stirred me, as though I had come to expect them as routine. Familiarity, while comforting, began to erode enchantment, which lost its magic the moment it became too predictable.

True wonder thrives on rarity, not routine.

But there was something more transcendent in the rediscovery of that curious, childlike state I had long left behind in my sprint to adulthood, something that subtly altered the course of my practice and life. It wasn't just about applying that beginner's mind to the world around me, though that was part of it. It was when I turned it inwards, towards the anarchy of my thoughts and restlessness, that something changed. In the introspective confrontation with myself, with my discomfort, I found a consoling courage. Not the kind of strength I thought I was supposed to have, but a stubborn kind that didn't come from certainty or confidence but from the willingness to sit with the unknown. And with that I realised the courage I had been searching for was never about running away from the darkness; it was about standing in it and not blinking. And the tool I used to navigate this darkness, the ally I brought into those places of fear and discomfort, was curiosity. When pain or overwhelm arose, instead of avoiding it, running from it, or distracting myself, I leaned in, curious, as if I were experiencing it for the first time. I would ask myself, '*Where do I feel this in my body? What thoughts, what emotions, and what sensations are there with it?*'

I approached it with the same wonder I had once reserved for the natural world as a child – the plants, the animals, the landscape. There was a softness in that approach, which balanced the moment's intensity and warmed the coldness of unease. I didn't want to escape it; I wanted to move towards it, learn more, stay open and remain inquisitive.

It always wasn't easy. There were moments in my meditations when things would rise inside me, suffocating equanimity. Vivid flashbacks would hit unbidden, dragging me down with the weight of shame's heavy chains. I'd become lost in a sea of ruin haunted by past mistakes, decisions that turned into regrets, the hurt I'd caused, or the hurt inflicted upon me. My mind would build elaborate future scenarios, each more ridiculous than the last, imagining myself fleeing to Alaska, living off the land in the wilderness as if some foolish choice demanded such an escape. And, as ever, with each of these mental spirals came an emotional charge, sometimes so intense it felt impossible to sit with. Over time, however, curiosity became the force that allowed me to weather these emotional surges. Rather than shy away from them, I began to ask questions, getting to know them, approaching them like unfamiliar ground, full of unknowns. For years, I had struggled in therapy to confront these parts of myself; now, I was immersed in them, approaching them with the same wonder a child feels when they stumble upon something completely new.

I refer to this as 'the novice soul', our third Polaris principle on this path towards the place that has never been wounded. The novice soul in meditation can represent a state of openness and curiosity, where the mind approaches each moment without preconceptions or attachments. It is the beginner's mind, unknowing yet eager to explore. This novice soul manifests as a willingness to observe thoughts, sensations and emotions without judgement or expectation. This curiosity fosters a deeper, more authentic connection to the self, creating space for insights and understanding to unfold naturally, each moment becoming a blank canvas, as the Taoists describe.

A particular memory used to rise, uninvited, as I sat in stillness to meditate, a familiar flicker dragging me back to a very specific point in time: my Leaving Cert exams. For the unfamiliar, that's the final trial by fire before we leave school in Ireland. If you ever meet an Irish person and mention it, chances are they'll still wince or confess to the odd nightmare. It leaves its mark. This memory lingers so vividly in my mind because of how physical it was, how utterly visceral. I remember sitting down for my English exam, already frayed at the edges, and noticing the exam paper beneath my hands had turned to something like damp paste, soaked by the steady stream of sweat pouring off my face. The hall was baking under the heavy June sun, and the idea of opening a window, as always, seemed unthinkable to the teachers, as if fresh air might somehow compromise discipline. Without permission, I bolted to the toilet, barely making it into the cubicle before collapsing into a full-blown panic attack. I desperately tried to muffle its noise to contain the rising terror, but I don't know if I managed.

That moment still found its way back to me in meditation. And I would try to shove it away every time.

But then something changed. I began to approach the memory differently, not as the panicked boy inside it, but as an objective observer, almost like watching a scene unfold in a film, detached but curious. I started to notice what it stirred in me: the tightening in my throat, the shallowing of my breath. Instead of recoiling, I acknowledged it: *'That's interesting.'*

I explored it, sat with it, and took the heat out of it. And in doing so, other fragments began to surface, pieces I'd long buried beneath the instinct to look away. I remembered the examiner appearing quietly in the bathroom, standing just beyond the cubicle door. He didn't ask questions. He said he'd wait, and I could finish the exam, even if it took hours after everyone else had gone. No judgement. Just presence. An unsaid understanding. Maybe he recognised something. Perhaps he'd been there too. Those glimpses of human kindness remain with me, especially in such moments.

That learning seemed to unlock a door, and a stream of memories and thoughts came that I hadn't expected: some gentle, some heavy. But I welcomed them all with the same beginner's spirit, with a novice soul, open and unarmoured, like someone seeing familiar things for the first time.

Another unexpected yet welcome by-product of weaving this Polaris principle into my practice was that it opened me up to understanding the pain and tragedy of others. For years, the fragility of my mind had kept me at arm's length from vulnerability, both mine and anyone else's. I would avoid conversations that might stir rawness and turn away from stories that explored the darker edges of humanity. The discomfort was too great; it unsettled me in ways I couldn't articulate. But as I grew more accustomed to sitting with my shadow self, what I call the darker parts of my mind, I drew myself almost magnetically to that same darkness and light in others. Where once I feared it, now I approached it – with curiosity. I had conformed to a world where the architects of 'normal' maintained rigid boundaries, drawing lines that separated those who fit within society's narrow view from those who didn't. Nowhere was this more evident than in the realm of mental distress where, instead of extending compassion or trying to understand, we institutionalised the suffering, hiding it away like inconvenient truths and attempting to solve social problems with medical solutions.

We often do the same with our own emotional needs – burying them in the dark, as if to acknowledge them would shatter the illusion of normality. As humans, we are varied and unique, but one common denominator that threads through the fabric of our existence is our vulnerability. It is the stitch that ties us together, the fragile line that makes us human. It's the gap in the armour, the soft spot in the heart. We are not invulnerable, no matter how much we try to build walls or wear masks. And in that, we are bound by something more meaningful than anything we can control: the certainty that we can be hurt, stumble and fall.

And maybe it's in that fragility that we find our most authentic strength. Pain and suffering do not discriminate: they come for all of us, sooner or later. In a way, it is the great equaliser of our shared existence. And it is in this shared vulnerability that something extraordinary occurs: connection. To sit with someone in their pain, to hold space for their grief or their fear, is an act of immense intimacy. There is no other moment like it. When someone opens up to you, lays their heart bare, and trusts you with the truth of their hurt, it is not just an invitation to empathise. It is an invitation to be *human* together. You don't flinch. You don't recoil. Because somewhere deep down, you know that, in some way, this could be you. It could be any of us. And that is a kind of suffering solidarity: the understanding that we are all just doing our best, with the same fragmented hearts, walking the same uncertain road.

In this space of mutual vulnerability, it's here that we truly meet one another, in the most honest and unguarded way.

To be clear, I'm not drawn to darkness for its own sake. I don't chase it, and I certainly don't romanticise it. What I'm saying is that I'm not afraid of it. I see it as a place where real connection can happen, where people drop the act. But that connection isn't exclusive to struggle. I feel it just as much in joy, beauty, and those small, steady moments of peace. I'm curious about the whole range of it – the human condition in all its shades. And I'm especially drawn to people who move through the world with a certain lightness, an ease that feels rare and magnetic.

This novice soul – this open, searching curiosity – pulled me back to Julia Leonard's story. It made me sense an almost urgent need to share it, to let the world see what I had seen. Because Julia, like so many others, had been abandoned by a society too afraid to bear witness to her pain. We recoiled from it, shied away from its intensity rather than leaning in with the open-minded compassion that might have saved her. Instead of seeing the humanity in her suffering, we turned away, and what followed, for me, stands as one of history's most significant failures: the great confinement, the institutionalisation of vulnerability itself. We took the fragile parts of ourselves that we couldn't understand and locked them away; not out of malice, but out of fear – fear of what we might find if we dared to look.

Julia was committed to St Loman's by her husband, the man she had once trusted and whom she had accused of infidelity – a truth later revealed to be all too real. Julia's life was shattered in ways no person should endure. Her children, her heart's very beating, were taken from her as if she were no longer a mother but a mere shell of a woman. For over twenty years she lived within those walls, a silent observer of the life that had been stolen from her, until she died 22 years later, of the kind of brokenness no doctor could cure, no medication could mend. And it was when we set out to exhume her body, to finally give her the peace she had been denied in life, we discovered the grim truth: Julia's grave, like 1,300 others, was marked only by a number. Her number was 339.

Like so many others, her life had been swallowed by the void of a society that refused to understand its failures. And this wasn't just Julia's story. It was the story of all those buried there, each with pain and suffering. They didn't fail society. They were failed by it. They were pushed aside and othered because their pain made people uncomfortable. Because their suffering was too uncontained, too real.

It's easy to run from the uncomfortable, the messy, the painful – most people would avoid this story because it feels too heavy, intense and depressing. But for me, it wasn't about the darkness. It was about what I saw in it. The humanity. The love. The heartbreak. There were people who were very unwell, but they were generally in the minority. The residents were mostly people who, for whatever reason, didn't fit into society. They did not fail society; society failed them. I could see this because I didn't fear the darkness. I was open to it. Curious, even. Just like I learned to be with my darkness: in meditation sitting with it, not turning away, but allowing it to reveal what was hidden; in that space, I found not despair but understanding – not sorrow, but connection. And that's where liberation lies – not in avoiding the dark places but in stepping into them, letting them show you something you couldn't see in the light. After all, the light doesn't exist without the dark. And if we're brave enough to look, listen and feel, the darkness becomes not a space of unease but of growth and learning.

The story isn't just one of tragedy, it's one of humanity. One of resilience. One of love that refused to die, even when the world tried to bury it. And that, I think, is what Julia and so many others have left behind: a story of strength, heartbreak and the truth that we are all just human in the end. And in that humanness, we are all connected. Julia's family showed fierce courage and determination to keep her story alive, even when the world had long turned its back. And from that act of defiance, more families began to step forward, each one with a story to share, each one painful testament to the lives lost in St Loman's, lives buried beneath a shroud of silence and neglect.

We will build a memorial wall on the very grounds of that graveyard, where the forgotten souls of so many rest. It will stand as a promise to those who were denied dignity in life, a way of offering them some measure of it in death. This wall is not just a memorial. It is a symbolic act, perhaps a commitment, a vow that we will fight to never allow such a travesty to happen again. A commitment to stand in the light of our shared humanity, face the uncomfortable truths, and ensure that no one is ever again buried under the weight of society's indifference.

In much the same way I once tried to outrun the parts of my history – those heavy, shame-laden chapters filled with regret and the weight of despair – society, too, has spent centuries running from its uncomfortable truths. This history and, indeed, the present, is no coincidence. It's a mirror of the internal battles we face. In my own life, I learned to face those shadows, to sit with them in meditation, and in doing so, I began to understand how my mindfulness practice seeped into not only my inner world but my work, my interactions and the mechanics of my daily existence. It became a superpower, this ability to approach life with curiosity and experience every pain, joy and unexpected twist as though I were a novice soul, new to the world, open to whatever came my way. It's a strange thing, that act of seeing the world with the wonder of youth, even when adulthood presses in with its sharp edges and burdens. But it softens life's challenges. It doesn't dismiss them but changes how we deal with them. It becomes a kind of compass, guiding us not away from difficulty, but through it.

As you move towards the place that has never been wounded, there will be bumps, obstacles and moments when it feels impossible to keep going. There will be times when emotional storms rise, when the world's weight threatens to derail and distract. But if you approach those moments with the mindset of a novice soul and with the same curiosity and openness you would bring to anything new, it shifts the experience. It doesn't eliminate the difficulty but allows you to move through it and sidestep the impulse to turn back, avoid it or run. Instead, it invites you to engage, to grow, to soften. And in that, you'll find not just resilience but a more profound sense of connection to the world, others, and, most importantly, to yourself.

Audio track

The soundtrack and guidance accompanying Chapter 3 was composed on a century-old Steinway piano so beautifully out of tune that it seemed to carry the weight of a thousand forgotten songs. I remember sitting there, playing with the keys, imagining the hands that had played before me; the compositions birthed in this very place. I wondered about its journey, the miles it had travelled, the rooms it had filled with music. From this reverence the piece emerged: a reflection of the piano's journey, crafted by the skilled hands of master artisans, and its history written in every warped string and crooked key. And, of course, it mirrors my path, both fractured and whole, of possibility.

There is something incredibly emotive about playing a piano like that; it is the sound of a broken instrument, yet it is much richer than one without a history, just out of the wrapper. It seemed as if the out-of-tune strings had their language, which told a story of past songs, yet they continued searching for new melodies.

This music, this broken and warped music, is a calling. An invitation to the shadows, a muffled request to get up and see what moves around in the dark. It proves that every trip is precious, no matter the wounds or gaps. There is something holy in the brokenness; it is an understanding that everything, even if damaged, has a story to tell. In listening, I hope you'll reconnect with that part of yourself – the novice, still wide-eyed, still brimful of curiosity and untapped potential; the explorer who sees the world with fresh eyes.

Chapter 4

The Credence Frequency

There is a ceaseless, intrinsic transmission between the body and mind – an intuitive, primal trust unspoiled by self-doubt, cynicism and uncertainty.

The credence frequency.

Static interference from the chaos and noise of our external world can diminish the signal.

But in the arms of presence, with the breath's cadence, we tune back into its resonance.

It has stood with you from day one.

An ally in arms, an inherent wisdom, a silent alarm.

Tune out to tune back in; an end to begin.

To trust again that native instinct that broadcasts within.

The credence frequency, this Polaris principle.

Let it chart your course.

In the refuge of meditation, as we move towards the place that has never been wounded, we trust that it knows the way.

On this path we inhabit the body fully. We tune our awareness to this frequency, a sense of coming home, a sense of agency.

When thoughts, emotions and feelings invite the mind on detours and cul-de-sacs, we summon it back to the refuge of our physical selves, grounded and attuned to presence, our purest essence, open and accepting of whatever sensations accompany each moment, without judgement.

We embody this Polaris principle of the credence frequency.

THE PLACE THAT HAS NEVER BEEN WOUNDED

I felt like a taxi driver with no car. Receiving a P45 before I started the gig. My body had been a warrior for so long, a loyal protector from a rogue mind. It was the engine that gave me purpose and meaning. But what happens when that engine stalls? When the vessel you've relied on keeps breaking down?

There is a peculiar terror in falling apart before you've even had the chance to begin. In my early twenties, when most were busy erecting the scaffolding of a future, I stood on the brink of a promising rugby career, only to watch the foundations crumble under its weight. One moment, I was lacing up boots with purpose; the next, I was staring at the silence that follows a dream as it quietly slips through your fingers.

When I recount the litany of injuries that led to my retirement, it almost reads like an American horror story; an endless string of misfortune and desperation, each chapter darker than the last. I was tossed from pillar to post, sent to some of the world's best minds in human physiology, all trying to explain why my body kept breaking down, especially when I was supposed to be in the prime of my athletic ability. In my teenage years, I don't remember ever being injured. I was invincible then, or at least I thought I was. But with each surge of anxiety, my body broke down like plaster from a weary old wall. Looking back, I see that as the first sign of my anatomy rebelling.

The call came not long after I returned from the under-21 World Cup in Sydney. It was from Leinster Rugby, one of Europe's elite teams and the goal I'd been working towards for years. This Leinster team I had idolised growing up was filled with many of my heroes, the men I had watched and hoped to be like one day. But there was a catch. They expected me to attend a pre-season match just days later against their local rivals, Connacht. I was empty, completely drained. I'd played every minute of every game at that World Cup, and as you'd expect when you're wearing your country's jersey, each game was brutally intense. But I had no choice. I played that game, and something went fundamentally wrong. It turned out to be a double hernia, and I spent the rest of that season in excruciating, chronic pain, living on anti-inflammatories and painkillers, too terrified to admit to my new employers that I couldn't do the job I had been hired for. Surgery was inevitable.

A few months after the surgery, when I thought I was finally on the mend, my body turned on me again. I ruptured my thigh muscle. Still, to this day, it is the most intense pain I have ever physically endured. It left a hole in the middle of my thigh where the muscle had come off the bone. I never sprinted again. When I did manage to get back on the field, the injuries didn't stop. I tore both my hamstrings. And then, in a brutal twist of fate, I nearly lost an eye when one of my teammates accidentally stamped on my face during a game.

When one of your own team stamps on your face, you need to re-evaluate your life choices.

Not a single expert I saw ever considered that maybe something else was at play, something beyond their carefully honed theories. Of course, it wasn't their area of expertise. They could measure my muscles, joints, tendons and biomechanics, but they couldn't see what was happening beneath all that: the hidden toll my mind had been exacting on my body for years. Not once did my coaches ever ask, 'Is everything all right with you?' When you were injured, you became excess to requirements, just another broken piece in the machinery left to stew in the rehab room like a misbehaving child sent out of class. There was no room for weakness or fragility. But the truth was that my body had stored so much unchecked trauma over the years that it just couldn't take it any more. Every muscle, every joint, every tendon, every ligament had been pushed to its breaking point.

THE PLACE THAT HAS NEVER BEEN WOUNDED

My nervous system was in a constant state of hypervigilance, alert to every threat, real or imagined. There was no peace, no calm. Every fibre of my being was on high alert, stretched tight with the tension and stress I carried. It was as if my body was bracing for an impact that never came; but that didn't matter: it was exhausted, suffocating under the weight of a pressure I was incapable of releasing. Every second of every day, I held on, white-knuckled. And eventually, it broke. My body just said *no*.

It was the cruellest wound of all: the one thing I had always leaned on, the one constant in my life, the thing I had trusted without question, had turned against me. It was like a partner, once devoted, once a sanctuary, had now become a stranger, cold and distant. The bond I thought was sacred, splintered. And in that moment, the trust was gone and irrevocably shattered. I could feel the resentment grow inside me like a slow poison. I began to loathe my body, as though it had deliberately betrayed me, as though it had conspired to destroy my career. The bond between mind and body, once an unspoken treaty, a primal alliance, had ruptured completely.

The years after my forced exit from the game became a strange, awkward dance with my body, a twisted game of tic-tac-toe. For so long it had carried me, battered and bruised by every sacrifice and every compromise I had made. But now, the balance of power had shifted. I'd spent years tending to it, trying to heal what had been broken, nurturing what was worn down, all in the hope that it might one day repay me but, in fact, now was the time to catch up with the debt I had been accumulating over all those years of adolescent sacrifice. Years that should have been spent running wild, lost in the recklessness of a teenage wasteland, but which instead had been consumed by the singular focus of a professional career. This commitment stole from me more than just time; it stole my chance to live, to experience the messy, anarchic beauty of those years.

I tumbled, almost desperately, between bouts of obsessive exercise – as though the very act of physical punishment could somehow convince me I was still an athlete – and stormy states of hedonism and insurrection. Both were attempts, in their way, to do the same thing: to run, escape and drown out the situation's cruel reality. One was a desperate sprint, the other a slow, intoxicating slide. But in the end, they both acted as a distracting dissonance between my body and mind. Each session and event became more warped, extreme and absurd than the last. Professional athletes often speak of the void left behind when the adrenaline of big games fades, how nothing ever quite matches that rush. I was lucky because I had music. The band. The stage. But even that felt like a watered-down version of it. It wasn't that same electric, heart-racing, skin-shivering pulse of competition.

The wake-up call came during a physiotherapy session for a lower back injury I'd sustained after attempting to jump off a stage at a music festival. I am sure the crowd had quite the epiphany when they witnessed my seventeen-stone frame blocking the sun as it fell from the stage. The physio worked on stretching my lower back and hamstrings, but they wouldn't move. They felt rigid, unyielding. My body was completely locked. There was a moment when he paused, looked at me with a hint of disbelief, and asked, 'Are you always like this?' The truth was, I couldn't remember ever being any other way.

A moment of clarity.

For years, I internalised the very things that hurt me most, those unarticulated bruises of experience that, lacking expression, took up a muted residence within me. I thought of Dr Edith Eger who once told me, in her straightforward and gentle way, 'Niall, expression is the opposite of depression.' I'd never learned how to express myself. I didn't even have the language to begin. So, I repressed. And in doing so, my body became the holding pen for all left unsaid and years of holding on. Retirement wasn't a betrayal by my body. Quite the opposite: it was trying to speak to me in its own tentative, physiological way. Perhaps to warn me. Maybe even to save me. But, as is so often the case with such truths, neither I nor anyone else was listening.

We live in a world utterly obsessed with the body yet profoundly disconnected from it. We are bombarded daily with images of the 'ideal' body, endless fitness trends, and blanket wellness advice from a multi-trillion-dollar industry, as if we are all some homogeneous species with cloned personalities and body types. Physical appearance has become the currency of social value, the indicator that guarantees success, admiration and self-worth. Yet, for all this visual obsession, we find ourselves estranged from the very thing we obsess over: our bodies. Strangely, we can admire (and often envy) bodies on screens, magazines and billboards while remaining almost wholly disconnected from the one body that genuinely matters: our own. This paradox lies at the heart of our modern malaise. We lionise the body as a symbol of success and worth, yet we treat it more like a machine to be tuned and repaired than a living, breathing partner in our existence. We prod and push our bodies towards ideals but seldom pause to ask how they feel, what they need, or what they might be trying to tell us. In a society saturated with self-optimisation, the body has become an instrument, a vehicle of late-stage capitalism, a means to an end rather than a home to inhabit, much like this ideology perceives the environment as something to be exploited for economic gain.

Consider this: the body, in its essence, is not merely a tool for achievement but an experience to be lived. And yet, how often do we treat it as such? How frequently do we allow ourselves to fully feel it, rest in its rhythms, and heed its quiet signals? Modern culture does not encourage this kind of attunement. Instead, it teaches us to manage, manipulate and mould our bodies to fit prescribed ideals. From punishing fitness regimes to crash diets and cosmetic enhancements, the message is clear: the body must be conquered, improved and displayed. And there is no end of access to information that allows us to push for that.

This focus on appearance has profound consequences. We become adept at ignoring our bodies' whispers: the tension that signals stress, the ache that asks for rest and the flutter of unease that begs for attention. Over time, these whispers turn into shouts, headaches, exhaustion and anxiety and, even then, we may fail to listen.

It is no coincidence that stress and burnout are so prevalent today. The faster life moves, the more we retreat into our minds, leaving the body behind as a footnote. And yet, the body cannot be silenced indefinitely. It speaks in the language of tight shoulders, shallow breaths and fatigue, all signs that we have strayed too far from ourselves. When we dismiss or disregard the body, we get caught between stations, unable to tune into any frequency of coherence. The belief that the body is just a conduit for the physical self is misguided. It can be the lens through which we can access and see our emotional and mental states. To tune out of that frequency cuts us off from a well of wisdom and knowing.

In an age of disconnection, fully inhabiting the body is an act of rebellion. It is a reaction against the pressure to perform, perfect, and be anywhere other than in the full spectrum of awareness. It is a declaration that we are enough not because of how we look or what we achieve, but simply because we exist.

This journey back to the body is not about fixing what is broken, as I attempted for too many years; it is about remembering what has been forgotten. And I don't want this to sound like it is as simple as reading an inspirational quote, and all of a sudden, we're fist-bumping and high-fiving. It's not a linear journey. It is about seeing the body not as an object but as a companion, a confidante, a home. I needed help and therapeutic guidance to move to that place: caring for the body and taking responsibility for it is profoundly optimistic and empowering, but when that care tips into obsession, or when the body is taken for granted, it can turn against us. I know this because mine did.

And that is where the Polaris principle of 'the credence frequency' comes into play. How do we establish a more coherent and lucid transmission between the mind and the body? How can we evolve beyond the crutch of modern technology to interpret our inner states? And how might we begin to view the body not as an adversary but as a trusted ally?

When I attuned myself once more to this frequency, I came to understand why, at some point, I had tuned out. In many ways, it was a self-preserving act and entirely understandable. Now, however, I relish exercise and physical challenges not as punitive acts or measures of worth, but as celebrations of movement and vitality. It allows me to spend extended periods in nature, where I am happiest. This transformative altering of my perspective changed the frayed relationship I had with my physical self. And a core component of this shift was deepening my practice. A daily inquiry and tuning in: *Is it best to rest the body today? Is there a tension, a holding within me that is attempting to communicate with my mind? Can I stretch my limits safely, or would restraint better serve me? Can I use movement to ground an unsettled mind, to create an anchor, a sanctuary?* This wisdom does not emanate from data points on watches or phones. It is not revealed through algorithms or notifications. Instead, it is uncovered through connection, intuition and, crucially, silence.

The body scan meditation is a powerful practice for fortifying the deep-rooted connection between body and mind. By directing awareness towards the subtle currents of sensation, emotion and the state of our physical being, and by embracing the Polaris principles of non-judgement and the openness of a novice soul, we begin to attune ourselves to this sacred frequency of resonance. In doing so, we learn to hear its wisdom and trust it implicitly, allowing its guidance to ripple through our awareness and restore harmony within. The mind no longer speaks *at* the body but *with* it. In that exchange, we find equilibrium, steadiness and, most importantly, a deep and abiding trust in ourselves. Perhaps, in reconnecting to our bodies, we have also reconnected to something far more significant: the rhythms of the earth and the essence of our existence. Our mind and body maintain a continuous dialogue, which extends to a deeper connection that reaches beyond our individual selves into the surrounding world. Our environment functions as an active participant, which produces a silent yet meaningful voice that shapes our well-being through an ongoing dialogue. The sacred trinity of communication between mind, body and nature grows stronger through active listening and engagement. Nature presents itself in its unadulterated form through a fundamental vibration that penetrates our being to calm our nervous system and still the continuous mental dialogue. The force of calm exists as a natural reinforcement, which we have known since ancient times yet we frequently forget. We will revisit this in future chapters. The earth exists as more than a surface beneath you.

And in this reawakening, we move closer towards the place that has never been wounded, body and mind, an alliance in purpose and direction.

Audio track

I composed the music and soundtrack for the credence frequency several years ago, a piece born from a deeply personal and poignant moment. It was inspired by my parents' 50th wedding anniversary, celebrated in the Great Northern Hotel in Bundoran, County Donegal, where their story began. It was here, amidst the innocence of their youth, that they first met.

They both danced together alone on the dance floor, one of the most moving experiences I have ever had. At that moment, they were not my parents but two teenagers greeting love for the first time. Their movements were soft, unhurried and steeped in intimacy; a language only they understood that had been crafted over half a century. They respected each other's bodies and cradled them; it was a life lesson from the people responsible for my existence. Love was woven into every subtle step, every gentle sway. The crowd faded into irrelevance; the room was theirs alone. Although their bodies had slowed since they had met in this location decades before, they still had the same affection and companionship. My siblings and I felt a great sense of gratitude that evening.

The music I wrote was also shaped by the words of one of the world's great philosophers, Alan Watts, who said, 'You don't aim at a particular spot in the room because that's where you will arrive. The whole point of the dancing is the dance.'[4] Witnessing my parents dance that night felt like something rare, something honest. It wasn't polished or rehearsed. It was a rhythm born out of years spent side by side, navigating life's highs and lows, the victories and the losses, and all the quiet, ordinary moments in between.

Their dance was about showing up again and again for each other. And as I watched, I realised I wasn't just seeing two people move their bodies gently to music. I saw love in its rawest form: resilient, evolving and steady enough to keep dancing, no matter what song life played next.

For the piano, I wanted it to feel like that gentle, flowing dance. The body moving in tandem with the mind, releasing itself from inhibition and holding, and, just like that night in the Great Northern Hotel, entirely in the moment. It's a moving piece of music that aims to represent that moment when the body and mind meet, reconnect, recognise each other and embrace.

The ambient meditation was constructed to create an awareness to explore the body within the body scan meditation. There are subtle, nuanced mechanical sounds of the piano in the background – the creaking of old piano stools, pedal movement, and the strings being released. It brings you closer; it invites you into this frequency of silence, where we can tune into the credence frequency.

Chapter 5

Grace

Sometimes you have to sing to yourself the lullabies no one else will. Be the mother, the friend, the lover you need in your darkest hours.
                                                                Unknown

A particular kind of restless energy creeps in whenever I hit 'record' for my podcast *Where Is My Mind?* – a jittery, electric hum that feels sharper now, more finely tuned, as if the edges have tightened over the years, pulling everything into a crystalline clarity. It's not the fear of unpreparedness, or the old ritual of second-guessing my knowledge that I used to flirt with before exams (though there is no lonelier place than to be stuck in an interview with your pants down around your ankles, not knowing what you are talking about), but more like a respectful reverence. I have been fortunate to sit across from and interview some of the most brilliant minds of our generation: Gabor Maté with his piercing insight into the human condition; Deepak Chopra's sage weaving of the spiritual and the scientific; Steven Hayes, a pioneer charting unmapped territories of the mind; and others whose work has influenced how I think and how I live. But there's this nuanced dance I must do, this delicate choreography with each interview, between staying present and not letting myself tumble headfirst into wide-eyed fascination.

I'll confess that dancing has never been my forte. That part of my brain seems a bit underfunded, always half a beat behind, moving with the elegance of a startled giraffe. But it's about holding on to myself, even as the conversation pulls me towards that edge where my personal agenda threatens to take over. I have to remind myself to stay grounded and open but remember that my role isn't to feed my hunger for insight; it's to gently mine their wisdom and carve out something meaningful for the listener.

Time is the enemy in these conversations. If I'm lucky, I have an hour, or an hour and a half if I push it and their publicist doesn't jump in to inform me with faux politeness that they have 'a hard out on the hour'. It's never enough. I always fear that I will forget something, not ask the right questions, or not pull a particular thread to the end.

These weekly collisions of thought can hack me or manipulate well-formed and often stubborn opinions. They aren't always comfortable. Sometimes, they can be a mind riot, and I spend the rest of the week attempting to restore peace. I touched on this earlier, in Chapter 2's 'Untethering', where I tried to capture how the most illuminating moments often emerge from unscripted, unplanned dialogues. It's in the push and pull of conversation, the rhythm of back and forth, opening the door to allow alternative perspectives or to defend your own. And I can't help but feel a certain amount of disillusionment at the thought of how critical thinking appears to be eroding from conversation. We have become so vested in our stories, so closed off to having our worldviews questioned.

For me, there's a strange energy in being mistaken, in watching the scaffolding of my beliefs buckle and fall apart. A new internal architecture emerges in those fractures, something sharper, vivid and sturdy. Being wrong isn't a failure; it's a chance to start over, to see things through a new lens. And there's a thrill in that process, a subtle satisfaction in the breaking and the rebuilding. When you hold the Polaris principles of non-judgement and the novice soul in your consciousness, it allows you to face these moments as a space of learning, rather than an infliction of destruction on our selves. In our contemporary cultural landscape, which seems to put more value on being first than being accurate or truthful, this is an act of defiance.

For a long time, education felt more like confinement than freedom to me. It was rigid, impersonal, a prison you had to endure, not something you looked forward to. But I have come to see it differently. Real learning is fluid. It's about keeping your mind and your heart open. It's about not holding on to your knowledge too tightly. I attempt to bring that to these conversational interviews: a willingness to be threatened and transformed. If there's one thing I've learned, it's that growth doesn't occur in the safe space, but in discomfort. It happens in the gaps and areas where we expose ourselves enough to listen.

When I interviewed Dr Kristin Neff for the podcast, it was one of those rare, charged moments that made me feel like stepping into a dialogue I wished could stretch forever. She's not just a self-compassion academic and globally celebrated leading researcher on the topic; she embodies it, lives it, and has fundamentally shifted how we define it. In fact, over 5,000 studies have been conducted on self-compassion by various scholars since Kristin's seminal papers were first published in 2003. I was in safe hands. She weaves the precision of science with the depth of human empathy and treats self-compassion not as an indulgence but as a core requirement.

And yet I took some convincing.

There is a reason, I suspect, that, for me, the word *compassion* always felt like it was trying on shoes two sizes too big: well-intentioned, slightly awkward, and never quite fitting me comfortably. It wasn't just a word; it was a trigger, a bruise I'd been poking at for years. It annoyed me, if I'm being honest. It felt slippery, overused, diluted by a thousand well-meaning but empty redefinitions. I'd seen it weaponised, too, in my own life and the lives of others. People hid behind it, claiming they were acting from a place of self-compassion when it was just insecurity or selfishness dressed up in spirituality-bypassing jargon. And I'd been guilty of that, too: no one likes holding up a mirror to their destructive behaviour. Compassion had become a word tangled in contradictions, and untangling it felt like trying to unravel a knot that got tighter the more I pulled.

I grew up steeped in a culture tangled in moral contradictions that twisted compassion into something soft, almost shameful; a trait to be hidden, not embraced. Tears, if they dared surface in a young man, were met with a kind of chastened violence, shoved back into the eyes they spilt from, as though the vulnerability was a flaw to be corrected. It was a world that taught me to armour myself and bury the things that might have set me free. This cultural conditioning seeped into me, becoming second nature, as if etched into my bones. It wasn't just the world outside that enforced it; my inner voice became its fiercest enforcer. I policed myself harshly and unrelentingly, as though the weight of those expectations had grown roots deep inside me. It was a trade-off: the world demanded I conform, and I, in turn, demanded it of myself, carving the same rules into my spirit.

As I moved through my studies, learning, fumbling, piecing things together, this word 'compassion' kept surfacing, like a half-remembered tune that insisted on playing in the background no matter how often I changed the station. It was inescapable: at retreats, in workshops and during lectures, inducing a labyrinth of fabricated fervour and, at times, deep frustration.

I devoured libraries of literature on the subject, dissected its definitions, and nodded along at its importance. On paper, I got it. In theory, I accepted it. But in practice? Something blocked me, some invisible wall I could not climb, no matter how many times I tried. I could intellectualise it, talk about it, even teach it. But 'feel' it? That was a different story. It was like trying to cuddle a cat that did not want to be cuddled: the more affection I offered it, the more it slunk off or clawed me.

Over the years spent guiding people through the curious art of mindfulness, I realised, with a certain sheepish relief, that this particular unease was not mine alone. And it's one of the main reasons people walk away from the practice altogether. Life experience, cultural conditioning, and the weight of it all can be so persuasive and loud that it leaves us punch-drunk. We throw in the towel, convinced we're just not cut out for it, instead of seeing it for what it is: not a failure, but part of the process. The mess, the resistance, the doubt: it's not the enemy. It's the work. And sometimes, the hardest part is just staying in the ring. In addition to this, the deeper societal swindle convinces us that our lives should always be easy and that happiness and contentment should fall into our laps without a struggle. It tells us we're owed a world free of discomfort, where every desire is met without effort and every need is fulfilled. It's a seductive lie that leaves us brittle and unprepared for the unembellished, messy and human truth that growth comes about from friction, and meaning is often born from the very things we'd rather avoid.

I had the unenviable task of presenting this line of thought to my esteemed guest, Dr Kristin, all while carrying the weight of not wanting to come across as if I were questioning her life's work. Far from it: I was reaching out to her expertise, experience and humanity, hoping for guidance, despite the slight, persistent guilt that always lingers when I do this. I have this uneasy feeling that I'm tapping into the wisdom of those who've spent their lives honing their particular knowledge, as if I'm taking something I haven't earned: free therapy. But then, I think, maybe that's the heart of what pulls people in.

The podcast emerges from my genuine unfiltered interest in the people I interview who share their wisdom and life experiences and the stories that formed them. The audience connects with me because I naturally gravitate towards the deep aspects of others. The process of listening becomes a shared discovery of truths because we experience those sudden moments of understanding, which feel like revelations and moments of clarity. That's the magic of it. A conversation transforms into a living entity that modifies you, even if only slightly, when it transcends mere words.

The podcast also isn't polished or rehearsed; it's unstructured, honest and unformulaic. And I could tell Kristin was relishing this. There was a spark in her, a subtle delight in being pushed and asked to dig deeper. Like me, she knows that honest doubt doesn't come from confrontation but from being challenged respectfully, even invigoratingly. This wasn't new territory for her, of course. I have always taken pride in asking questions that may not have been asked before, the kind that make someone pause and think. That's the sweet spot in a good interview: when you can practically hear the cognitive processing; when the pauses are as meaningful as the answers. That's the moment you're aiming for. And when you get it, there's nothing like it.

There is a reason that Kristin is considered the global authority in self-compassion. The leaders in her field, the real experts, don't just break the surface. They don't see things in one dimension. They immerse themselves in exhaustive research, the nuances, the complexities and the often-shifting dynamics of the subject. They observe it with an objective detachment, no matter if the territory is complicated and charged with emotions.

And she didn't let me off the hook – not that I expected her to.

She challenged me when I told her I struggled to feel compassion for myself. 'You wouldn't do what you do,' she said, 'if you didn't care deeply. Not just for others, but for yourself too.'

I conceded the point but added that offering that compassion to others had always felt easier than turning it inwards.

She had heard that a thousand times before and did not seem surprised. But then she asked: 'What comes to mind when you hear the word "compassion"?'

That set me off on some chaotic mental gymnastics. And I realised the word triggered a strange, almost childlike visualisation: pastel colours, soft and light, like something out of a cartoon. And, weirdly (though let's be honest, I've never claimed to be 'normal' in this book), my mind drifted to the Teletubbies. Yeah, those odd, babbling creatures from kids' TV. In my head, it was as if we reserved compassion for babies. For the fragile, the innocent and those in need of protection. I don't know why that was my first instinct. Maybe there's some Freudian psychoanalytic rabbit hole to dive into, some deep-seated reason buried in my subconscious. But honestly? I didn't care to dig that deep. Sometimes, a thought is just a thought, and a Teletubby is just a Teletubby. But what it did reveal was that there was a perception of silliness and childishness to the word for me.

On top of all that, my relationship with the word, shaped by my upbringing, my social conditioning, and all those invisible forces that mould us without asking, triggered something that often drowned out any chance of offering kindness to myself. The word hijacked my inner world, commandeered the main stage, and turned itself into the headliner. Everything else, even basic self-respect, got relegated to the support act, barely audible over the noise. And the thing about headliners? They don't leave much room for anything else. They demand all the attention and energy until you're left wondering why you can't just tune them out and let the quieter, gentler voices have their moment. But life, as I've learned, rarely works that way.

Kristin's suggestion was one of those beautifully simple yet radically obvious ideas that make you wonder why you hadn't thought of it.

'So it's not the feeling,' she said, 'it's the word. Why don't you use another word?'

It wasn't about ditching the concept of compassion. It was about finding a word that didn't trigger all the noise and pastel-coloured Teletubby baggage.

Often, the most significant shifts come from the smallest tweaks, and Kristin, with her compassionate wisdom, had just handed me the key to a door I hadn't even realise was locked.

I took a lot from my privileged time with Kristin. I discovered that 'compassion' is not a foreign idea to me, and I realised that language – those carefully crafted, persuasive words – can sometimes drown out what we already know to be true. A small but steady spark exists within us, then language comes along, a can of fuel in hand, and pours itself over everything. Before you know it, the flame roars, and by the time you've put it out, you are too exhausted to clean up the mess.

In the fire's aftermath, I needed words that worked with the feeling, not against it. Words that felt right for me. I needed something deeper, that carried both vulnerability and strength, kindness and responsibility, mercy and clemency. A word I could hold on to without turning it into a weapon, without twisting it into some faux self-care mantra while secretly being a bit of a dick. I needed a word that wouldn't just sound good but would *feel* good. A word I could embody in those moments when life decides to thump you square in the face, and instead of raising your hands to shield yourself, you use yourself as a punching bag.

I thought about those times, those turbulent, ugly moments where the abuse I hurled at myself was relentless, unyielding. All I ever needed was someone in my corner to fight that fight with me or, at the very least, help me off the canvas when I was flat on my back.

That word was 'grace' – a word you can feel as you say it.

GRACE

'Grace' is the rendering of kindness, understanding and forgiveness to ourselves, especially in times of failure, struggle or imperfection. It is about offering empathy to ourselves as we would a friend when we need it most. Grace recognises our flaws, our fallibility, our fragility. It's not a license to make excuses for failures or shirk responsibility. It is something we carry and offer to others. It is an absence of entitlement and expectation. It's the realisation that when your world falls apart, it's not always correlated to something you did or did not do. Grace is the space you make for yourself when you feel unsteady, uneasy and unsure. It is both powerful and tender. It is the liberation of realising that you don't always have to keep up with the demands of a world out of control.

Grace feels spiritual. It recognises that we are all connected and we all need each other.

Not long after my conversation with Kristin, I found myself in the thick of one of the most challenging periods of my life, both professionally and personally.

Professionally, I was dropped, like third-period French, by three of the entities I worked with. In the creative industry, your security is only as solid as your last and next commissions. I'm no stranger to the risks. I'm a big boy; I know how it works. These dry spells happen. But being let go by a record label, a podcast platform and a publisher all within a few months? That felt particularly brutal.

In moments like these, you're supposed to play the game. Smile, nod and post some polished LinkedIn drivel about 'moving on to fresh pastures' or 'exciting new opportunities'. Never let them see you sweat. But this time, I didn't want to play along. I wanted to be honest and live what I teach. So, I posted the truth on my social media: I got dropped. One of the three previous employers sent me a massive bunch of flowers, which I found hilarious. My mum was thrilled when I passed them on as a gift, so I guess some good came of it. But the truth? I was hurting. My worth felt like it was under a microscope, and I was drowning in self-doubt and insecurity. The financial pressure was overwhelming – mortgages and a dog with a gourmet appetite don't pay for themselves.

On top of that, family issues were simmering in the background, making everything feel heavier. In the past, I would've carried it all alone, as I had a pathological habit of shouldering the world without asking for help. But this time, I had Louize, my long-term partner, the strongest woman I've ever known.

Even then, it was hard to let her in. Old habits die hard. I told her, 'I'm going to feel all of this. It hurts to be rejected like this.'

I stepped back. I allowed myself to sit with the car crash, the fear, the uncertainty, the gritty edges of it all. And through it, I offered myself grace. Each day, in meditation, I'd repeat, 'This hurts. This is tough. I offer myself grace, and I let it in.' My hand would rest on my chest, and I'd feel the words ease my spirit.

I'm unsure if I'd have made it through if I were still wrestling with the word 'compassion'.

A few months later, I sensed the apathy lifting, that familiar spark of intrinsic motivation flickering back to life. The kind that makes you willing to risk failure again, to dive into new work despite the fear of falling flat on your face or rejection. (During times like these, I advise people to steer clear of those social media platforms where tech bros hold court, spouting endless strategies for success and prosperity. Where earnest emotive piano motifs swell into crescendos with the roar of the orchestra, and perfectly curated reels make you feel like Rab C. Nesbitt munching on a Toblerone and rewatching *South Park* reruns.) I started to craft new creative

GRACE

ideas, developed them, and formulated them into something that I could pitch. Hopefully, people would be interested in.

But there was a hesitation.

I would write emails to my agent, Glenn, and attach the files and then freeze, unable to click 'send'. It's almost impossible not to doubt yourself after being let go so abruptly and repeatedly. That kind of rejection leaves a mark, and suddenly, showing people your work feels like doing a bungee jump with some dodgy, backyard operator. Instead, I would show these ideas to my friends and family, who, given the shitshow I had gone through, out of love would have called me a genius if I even sent them a kazoo performance of 'Mary Had a Little Lamb'. Rejection makes you doubt everything, including the work you know is good. Sometimes, the most challenging part is not the creation but the send button.

Finally, I found the courage to press 'send'. Months later, that one act led to signing the most significant audio commission of my career: one that didn't just tell a story but sparked something bigger, something with a genuine social impact.

And then, as if the universe was nodding, I signed the deal for the book you're holding now.

And *you're* reading this book because you have the same bravery and courage. You're willing to step into the inner world. A place that can feel terrifying, confusing and utterly overwhelming at times. And as we walk this path together, towards that place within us that's never been wounded, there will be moments when you'll need to pause, put your hand on your heart, and offer yourself grace. Offer yourself the respect you deserve.

Let's be honest; most people don't do this work. They look for the bypass, the short cut, the easy way around the hard stuff. But not you. You're taking the scenic route, and there are no short cuts here. But if you carry these Polaris principles with you: non-judgement, untethering, the novice soul, the credence frequency and grace, they'll guide you when you feel lost.

THE PLACE THAT HAS NEVER BEEN WOUNDED

The world throws a lot at us. And if you're like the majority, when it does, you tend to see yourself as the reason for the chaos. But the world is complex, layered and pretty damn random. Sometimes, accepting that we're not to blame for every failure nor solely responsible for every triumph makes offering ourselves grace much easier. It's not about letting yourself off the hook, but realising you were never on it.

Audio track

I composed the music for 'Grace' to carve out space. Space for the words to land, to be felt and heard. Like the first piece leading into the Polaris principles, there's a simplicity to it. It's meant to mark the end of Act 1, to honour the journey we've taken to get here.

The chord progression is warm and inviting, designed to mirror the sentiment of grace. The organ lends a spiritual, almost sacred quality, as if it's reaching for something beyond the everyday. The music should feel strong yet vulnerable, as if it offers mercy, clemency – and a soft place to land.

This meditation often stirs something emotive in people. Letting grace in, genuinely feeling it, can crack things open. And that's okay. Let it all in. Hold it gently.

Act II

Dúchas

Dúchas is a Gaelic word that holds fast our bond to land, story and bloodline, declaring who we are with the instinctive certainty of belonging. It is the steady pull that keeps you rooted, even when life tries to scatter you. The unseen hand that shapes you, the voice that calls you home when the world has made you a stranger to yourself.

Act II turns us inwards, towards the mind's expansive, shifting landscapes, the spirit's restless stirrings, and the invisible threads that tie us to our environment. It asks more than a glance at the self; it draws us into the places that have shaped us; into the breathing, moving life that evolves around us. Here, the land is no longer a backdrop but a guide. Its cycles remind us of change and renewal, its stillness invites reflection, and its fortitude teaches strength. In its rhythms, we begin to see the possibility of our wholeness mirrored back to us. *Dúchas* reminds us that by deepening our relationship with the land, we deepen our relationship with ourselves.

The land I evoke in Act II draws its breath from the Irish landscape surrounding me. It is a place rich with old stories, fierce beauty and lessons, if you are willing to listen. In the world of the early Irish pagans, land and spirit were one. Mountains, rivers and forests carried presence and meaning, shaping not only the world they lived in but the lives they led. They moved with the seasons, listened to the wind, and found in the land a patient teacher rather than something to be used, tamed or overcome. To them, honouring the earth was honouring themselves — a reflection of what *dúchas* teaches: that belonging is both born and remembered through the living bond between people and place.

We have built new gods in modern life: endless growth, relentless productivity and prosperity at any cost. Modern culture has shaped our actions and values, individually and collectively, reducing the environment to a resource, something to be exploited rather than experienced. Climate change, the greatest existential threat humanity faces, remains a footnote in global priorities. It reveals how far we have drifted from the land that once grounded us. And this disconnection echoes the split between body and mind I spoke of in Act 1, through the credence frequency — the same fracture, but now evident between ourselves and the natural world.

Yet some bonds cannot be broken. The relationship between humans and nature remains written in our bones. Countless studies show what we already feel: nature restores, heals and holds us together.

This is why the natural world sits at the heart of mindfulness meditation, as a reminder of the old relationship that has always sustained us, even when we forgot how to honour it. Mountains, rivers and the vast unbroken sky are not backdrops to our lives; they are reflections of life's impermanence, the ground beneath all our passing moments. Is there any wonder why more and more healthcare professionals are now prescribing eco-therapy: time spent walking in forests, tending gardens, or simply being outdoors? Backed by research from journals like *The Lancet* and by national programs such as PaRx in Canada and green social prescribing in the UK, it shows how nature powerfully eases anxiety, lifts depression and restores both body and mind.

One weekend, we had been kayaking for six relentless hours, fighting the angry, heaving waters. Each stroke felt heavier than the last. The wind, never our friend, had lashed at us the whole way, and I was done. A broken man with an aching back and a vocabulary that would offend a drunken sailor.

One of my comrades, Dav, chose that precise moment to lift our spirits. 'Did you know,' he called over the roar of the lake, 'that a boat carrying hundreds of barrels of Guinness went down right about here? Took a fair few poor souls with it, too.'

Ah, Dav. A master of consolation.

Ahead lay the final stretch: twelve gruelling kilometres to Killaloe in County Clare. The home stretch, but it felt insurmountable. The weather, a moody Irish cliché, had been against us all day. I clenched my jaw, trying to keep my misery to myself. We were all in the same boat. Exhausted. Emotional. Fractured versions of ourselves.

Then, something rare happened. The wind shifted direction. As if the lake had made a decision, it reversed. A north wind rose from nowhere, catching our backs and pushing us forward. The water shifted, lifted and rolled beneath us, not in fury but in support. Then, with seemingly divine illumination, the sky exploded open; the clouds that had been sitting on the lake in a gloomy, misty manner for days burst to reveal something we thought we might never see again: the sun. It was as if Mother Nature had felt sorry for this group of sorry kayakers and put her arms around us.

Act II gathers five chapters of meditation, spoken word and reflection, each one rooted in the vivid ideas of nature, beauty and truth. It allows us to recognise our inner landscapes' transience, and find meaning in their shifting forms.

6. Be the Lake

I grew up in County Westmeath, in the Midlands of Ireland's hidden heartlands – a place of broad flatlands and open fields, stitched together by striking lakes and endless bogs, cradled by the earth and shaped long ago by the slow hand of glaciers. It is a land that has rested, unbothered, for centuries.

The lakes shaped life around them. During the darkest moments of my youth, they became my lifeline. They were my therapist, mentor and closest friend. I knew every inch of their shorelines, every curve and hidden cove. Years later, while studying mindfulness, I was introduced to the practice of 'lake meditation'. I finally understood what those lakes had been trying to teach me in the bedlam of my youth.

Lough Ennell, Lough Owel and Lough Derravaragh had always been speaking; I just hadn't been ready to listen.

I think back to those days, standing on their shorelines. Some days, the water was so still it seemed you could step out onto it. The sky, mirrored perfectly on the surface, made the world feel endless – a strange, almost psychedelic stillness, where water and sky dissolved into each other and the edges of things disappeared. On other days, the lakes churned like the North Atlantic in storm season – wild, chaotic, impossible to predict. And in winter, when the frost tightened its grip, they froze solid, rigid beneath the heavy cold. You could even walk across them, if you dared.

Whether the lakes raged under storm clouds or lay still as glass, something was always shifting beneath the fluidity of the surface. And in that consistency, the loughs taught me more than any book ever could.

I learned to 'be the lake' – to hold space for change, weather the storms and recognise the constancy within myself.

7. Be the Mountain

The second chapter of Act II turns to the teachings of mountain meditation.

When you observe a mountain, you feel its immensity at once. Rising from the earth's bedrock, its vast, unshakable mass carves into the sky. Yet year after year, it bears the slow violence of the seasons – heat splitting its surface, frost driving into its cracks, storms and snow grinding it down. Still, the mountain endures. Although its surface shifts with the seasons, its core remains steady and unmoving.

The mountain meditation mirrors this inner life: a shifting landscape of thoughts, emotions and changes moving through us like weather across stone. And yet beneath it all, something remains steady, grounded, untouched.

This is the heart of the practice. We learn to 'be the mountain'.

8. Be the Sky

When my anxiety was at its most unruly, panic attacks lurked behind me like a shadow, and my thoughts hurled themselves at each other like overexcited teenagers at a Slipknot gig: frantic, graceless and wholly uninterested in reason. My world would shrink, growing unbearably small and suffocating. It wasn't merely a trick of the mind; it was savagely physical, like being seized by some invisible brute I had no hope of wrestling free from. It felt like a possession at times, leaving me drained of any fight. But as I began to navigate recovery, mindfulness, over time, offered me something I hadn't felt in years: space.

The metaphor of the sky gave me a way to understand this. Living in Ireland, the skies rarely stay clear. But my world feels expansive and panoramic on those few summer days when the clouds vanish and the sky stretches out in blistering blue. I can breathe deeply in that vastness. And then, inevitably, the clouds return – dark, brooding, splintered, or those maddening days when the weather can't quite make up its mind. We might think of this as a reflection of the mind's endless habit of overproducing thoughts.

The practice isn't about chasing the clouds away or pretending they're not there. It's about learning to become the sky – to make room for all of it. You no longer lose yourself in the squall when you become the sky. You watch the clouds drift past. The world unfurls again. Your mind clears a space and, almost without noticing, you realise you are no longer trapped; your world is no longer tight and suffocating, but vast, open and infinite.

9. Be the Beauty

Chapter 9 in Act II takes us into the unfolding experience of discovering beauty in the mundane. It challenges our narrow, often superficial notions of beauty and invites us to broaden its meaning.

In a culture moving at relentless speed, where many of us feel we're barely keeping up, it's easy to slip into autopilot to survive. In that mode, life blurs – a chaotic monotony, a dull, monochrome canvas of routine and overwhelm. But when we do pause, when the noise begins to settle, we start to see beauty in the ordinary – not as an exception, but as omnipresent. As W. B. Yeats wrote, 'The world is full of magic things, patiently waiting for our senses to grow sharper.'

The spoken-word reflection that accompanies this chapter is brought to life by the ethereal and arresting voice of Noírín Ní Riain, one of the most powerful souls I've ever encountered. She embodies something ancient and unmistakably Irish: a fierce, feminine energy rooted in wisdom, compassion and melodic spirituality that feels both grounding and transcendent.

When she – a theologian, a singer, a keeper of old songs and older truths – speaks, it's less performance, more invocation.

This chapter isn't just about noticing beauty – it's about embodying it. When we learn to 'be the beauty', we don't just change how we see the world; we change our relationship with it. We begin to move towards something more whole, more human, and closer to that part of us that has never been wounded.

10. Be Your Truth

Growing up in Ireland in the 1980s and 1990s, the air we breathed carried the weight of one truth: the Catholic Church held the moral and ethical reins of the nation. Its authority was persuasive, unquestioned, and as solid as the stone walls of the cathedrals that climbed over the skylines of the towns and cities. For generations, we were told what to believe, what to feel, and even how to feel it. Agency wasn't ours to hold; it was rationed, monitored, confined. But beneath that fortress of faith lay a rot we would come to see for what it was: a systematic and devastating abuse of power that shattered lives and silenced souls.

But this chapter is not about faith. I will always respect people's faith and what brings them comfort. This is about the institution of the Church.

Over time, what once seemed unshakable began to crumble. The Church's grip faltered under the weight of its sins, leaving behind a vast, gaping silence where its moral compass had once stood. Into that vacuum poured something else: a new belief system built on materialism and wealth. The sermons of salvation gave way to sermons of success, measured not in piety but in possessions. Consumerism became our cathedral; luxury goods, our holy relics.

In this whirlwind of shifting values, it was easy to lose your footing. What do you believe when belief itself has become a currency to trade? What do you stand for when one generation's altar becomes the next generation's scrapyard? This wasn't just a shift in ideology, it was a moral whiplash – its sudden turns and plunges leaving us breathless, disoriented, and asking, 'Where do we go from here?'

We lost not only the Church but something more challenging to name: a thread that once tethered us to a shared sense of purpose. In that loss, we faced the daunting, liberating challenge of starting over, of deciding for ourselves what it means to live well, love fully, and stand for something that feels real. From a personal perspective, I felt unmoored, drifting without any clear sense of direction. My values became chameleon-like, shifting depending on the room I was in, taking on the colour of my surroundings. It wasn't deliberate, more a reflex, a way to blend in, to belong. I suppose that's part of being human, this instinct to adapt, to find a place within something larger than ourselves. But the jarring thing was that I felt utterly lost, even among those groups where I'd bent myself to fit. I didn't know what I stood for, what mattered to me, or what was real. The more I tried to find a foothold, the less stable the ground seemed. It wasn't that I didn't care; I didn't know where to start. It's unsettling to realise that the values shaping your life might not even be your own, but ones you've borrowed to survive.

A teaching from the Buddha's *Kalama Sutta* (loosely paraphrased) advises:

> *Do not go upon what has been acquired by repeated hearing, nor upon tradition, nor upon rumour, nor upon scripture, nor upon surmise, nor upon axiom, nor upon specious reasoning, nor upon bias towards a notion that has been pondered over, nor upon another's seeming ability, nor upon the consideration, 'The monk is our teacher.' When you yourselves know: 'These things are good; these things are not blameable;*

these things are praised by the wise; these things, when undertaken and practised, lead to welfare and happiness,' – then you should engage in them.

This teaching boils down to a simple, yet honest, truth: you are your authority.

We spend so much of our lives looking outwards and searching for validation, acceptance, or a sense of belonging in the values and morals of others, but the real work, the harder work, is tuning in to our own sense of morality and agency.

What truly matters to you?

What do you stand for, beneath the noise of expectations and assumptions?

Once you uncover that – and trust me, it's a process that often requires guidance (it certainly did for me) – you develop an internal navigation system. A compass that doesn't rely on external maps or borrowed directions. It doesn't mean you'll never feel lost again, but it means that when you do, you'll have something steady within you to guide the way.

This chapter will be about reflecting on that idea and grounding ourselves in our truth. It's a moment to pause, to sit with what we've uncovered so far, and to carry it towards that deeper place – the part of us that has never been wounded.

For this reflection, I'm honoured to share the voice of my friend, teacher and mentor, Michael Harding. His spoken-word piece for this chapter, accompanied by music, touches something in me that few others ever have. His words have guided me through moments of confusion and clarity alike. Having him as part of this journey is more than a privilege; it's a gift I'm grateful to share with you.

Chapter 6

Be the Lake

If you wandered a couple of miles in any direction from the front door of my childhood home, the shorelines of Lough Ennell, Lough Owel and Lough Derravaragh would soon greet you. This trinity of lakes has held me in my fear on so many occasions that I should compensate them for their unsolicited but deeply appreciated therapeutic interventions. Alas, incessant tributes and compliments regarding their significance will have to suffice.

Lough Ennell's Polaroid appeal hides a history and mystique that matches its alluring aesthetic. The inspiration behind the literary masterpiece *Gulliver's Travels* came from Jonathan Swift's regular retreats to the lake. The legend goes that while taking a boat trip across it, he watched the locals wave him off from the Lilliput shore (then called 'Nure'), and their diminishing size mesmerised him as the boat moved across the lake. Some whisper that Swift's inspiration might have been more psychedelic in nature, stemming from the bountiful harvest of liberty cap magic mushrooms that adorned the surrounding fields. Whether borne from the enchantment of perspective or the treasure of nature's kaleidoscopic bounty, the legend of *Gulliver's Travels* finds its roots entwined with the mysteries of Lough Ennell's shores.

You'll stumble upon Lough Derravaragh, the reputed playground for the misfortunate Children of Lir, a few miles northwards. Lore has it these children whiled away a staggering 900 years as swans, all thanks to the wicked machinations of their evil stepmother, Aoife. She, clearly in desperate need of some 'alone time' with King Lir, decided to hex the poor kids to a swan's existence to keep them off her back, only for the sound of a Christian church bell to break the spell.

Whoever created that tale may have been sampling the same local fungi as Mr Swift.

The Hill of Uisneach, steeped in myth and history, is nestled between the lakes and revered as Ireland's spiritual and geographic centre. It hosted ancient druidic rituals and was where the five provinces of Ireland converged. Legends speak of the Cat Stone, marking Ireland's centre, and the Lia Fáil, crowning high kings. It was home to Beltane fires and the resting place of Ériu, the goddess who gave Ireland its name. Uisneach remains a symbol of connection – more than just a hill – between land, legend and spirit. Anyone who has stood on it has talked about the healing energy reverberating through it. I believe that energy descends to the lakes.

Which would be why I was so magnetised to them in times of darkness, particularly in the shadowy haze of adolescence.

The humid late-summer sun had beamed through my bedroom window for most of the day. The tattered posters of Pearl Jam, Nirvana and Red Hot Chili Peppers were losing their grip on the walls of what felt like a steam room. The dead, inescapable heat, mixed with the unmistakable whiff of pubescent sweat, masked by a half-can of Lynx Africa, carried the pungent note of closing time at an overcrowded teenage disco. My neighbour's lawn mower, a decade overdue a service given the racket it was making, bellowed outside my window, the rattling ruckus distracting me from the surging sound of my frenzied breathing. I wrestled with my saturated bedsheets, attempting to anchor myself so I could catch enough breath to stop the suffocation. I captured a glimpse of my contorted body in the long mirror at the end of the bed, reminiscent of a frame plucked from a James Wan movie. It was as if someone had walked into my bedroom and aggressively placed a pillow over my face, and the more I struggled, the more they pushed down. Time itself felt as if it had been devoured by a voracious black hole, leaving me to watch my impending doom unfold, utterly immobilised and unable to intervene.

Your first panic attack is a permanent scar on the psyche. There is a powerlessness to it that forces you to acknowledge the reality of your fragility. In its wake, an insidious spectre looms: the constant dread of its inevitable return, an ever-present shadow lurking in the recesses of the mind. Yet it feels like it's at the core of your existence – anxiety on legs.

After a thrilling zero hours of sleep and a banging cortisol hangover, I embraced the settling relief of early morning's cool breeze coming through the bedroom window, a welcome reprieve from the languid humidity. In a groggy haze, I couldn't shake the suspicion that maybe the whole ordeal had been a wild lucid dream cooked up by my sleep-deprived, sun-stroked brain. But I kept the craziness to myself: honestly, I had no idea what I would say – an absence of language born out of a lack of comprehension.

Instead, I hopped on my bike and pedalled to Ladestown on the northern shores of Lough Ennell. My bike was a spray-painted hand-me-down from my brother, masked as a pretty shit Christmas present from my parents that, like my neighbour's prehistoric lawn mower, needed a bit of a service, but it just about got me there.

Turn right as you enter Ladestown, and you'll find a cul-de-sac that morphs seamlessly into a verdant forest teeming with life. One constant challenge with the lakes of Westmeath is the swarms of flies that revel in humid summer air and pasty Irish skin, but it's a small price to pay for being in the lake's presence.

THE PLACE THAT HAS NEVER BEEN WOUNDED

When we were kids, my parents and their friends would haul us out to Lough Ennell for picnics, where they'd unwind with cheap boxed wine while we roamed the shoreline. That forest had always claimed my imagination. Navigating the narrow paths, dodging the razor-sharp brambles and nettles, you'd eventually stumble upon a hidden cove.

This solitary spot, encircled by reeds and a resting place for many a swan, almost seems detached from the rest of the lake. No matter the conditions on the water, and they can get rough, there is always a harbouring consistency with the waves as they are welcomed to shore here. The surrounding trees mute the noise of the world and, at the same time, tune you into the frequency of nature. There is a small oval space of sandy soil, with two rocks offering themselves as seats on the water's edge.

For whatever reason that day, this was the place I felt I needed to come to. I propped my rusty ride at a gate leading into the forest. That is the virtue of having a battered bike: it's theft-proof, so there is no need for a lock, and if anyone did fleece it, they were welcome to it. My heart was still thundering – part panic, part pedalling – as I wound along the forest's faded old trails. I came across the legacy of a bonfire along with some crumbled cans of cheap lager and mounds of cigarette butts, and hoped whoever was shitty enough to leave this mess here was long gone. My brother Ronan used to regale me with tales of the hedonistic revelry he and his motley crew enjoyed there; a band of merry delinquents who, with admirable self-awareness, dubbed themselves 'The Extravaganza Club'. I remember my parents as not considering it particularly extravagant.

Arriving at the cove, I was relieved to see I was its only occupant. Over the years, I've frequented this cove countless times, uncovering something previously unnoticed with each return. The early morning sun creeping through the trees spotlit the flies, getting ready to cause mayhem on any human skin that came their way. The Japanese call this spectacle of light *komorebi*, sunlight sieved through leaves, a fleeting kind of magic. A beige froth clung to the shoreline, like someone had mischievously tipped a bottle of washing-up liquid into the lake. The muted sound of the water merged with the forest's acoustics as I took my place on one of the rocks, letting the stillness greet me like *shinrin-yoku*, the forest bathing I'd read about but never named until now.

The sky was almost indistinguishable from the azure blue of the lake. For the first time since the revulsion of my inaugural panic attack, I was coming to terms with what had happened. The initial shock had faded, and all that was left was a terrified and confused teenage boy sitting on the edge of a lake that he, for whatever reason, found comfort in. A rigid tension gripped my body, a palpable holding as if bracing for the impact of a slow-moving car. My shoulders were hunched around my neck, my jaw clenched, and my fingers raw from being restlessly rubbed together. I attempted to close my eyes, but this only induced flashbacks of the previous night.

Removing my trainers, I placed my feet into the refreshingly cool water, simultaneously jolting and calming my frayed central nervous system. Dragging my foggy consciousness to the lake's soundtrack, I tuned into the muffled sound of a distant boat engine, the birds chanting in the forest, the half-breeze in the reeds; and, for the first time since the cauldron of chaos that was the night before, I sensed cautious ease. In this truce, as the bolt of tension left my body, I started to sob silently, with the sobering realisation that the youthful innocence I had perhaps taken for granted was now corrupted.

Later, I wandered back to my bike, mildly hopeful that someone might've done me the favour of stealing it. But no, there it stood, precisely where I'd left it, as unappealing to thieves as ever. *Not even worth nicking*, I thought, with a sort of reluctant admiration for its steadfast uselessness.

That day sealed my lifelong kinship with the lakes. Indeed, this relationship has only strengthened with time, testament to the Irish landscape's capacity to heal those fortunate enough to experience it. It has held me in my darkest moments – though I have been fortunate to learn from many remarkable teachers, none have imparted wisdom or left as profound an impact as the lakes and the encompassing Irish landscape that hosts them. It was serendipity that they would later become a cornerstone of my mindfulness practice, years after they first wrapped their arms around me, when I needed to be held.

The room began to shed the noise and demands of the outside world. As the group settled into their space and assumed their meditation positions, the inviting voice of our teacher, Helen, enveloped the room.

In the early days of my mindfulness practice, I felt a deep envy for those impossibly pliable souls who folded into the perfect lotus position, as if their hips had been crafted by a benevolent yoga deity and not, as in my case, by a unskilled furniture maker – my professional rugby days had put an end to that aspiration. My knees, hips and ankles have been twisted, shattered and battered one too many times to attempt anything more than a good, old-fashioned sitting on the plush padding of one's own arse. But meditation is not a performance or a self-righteous opportunity to post your perfect practice across social media platforms. It is an opportunity to connect with a deeper part of yourself that transcends the shackles of expectations, those that often come with presenting the everyday self to our professional, social and personal world. When I caught myself casting a mildly resentful eye to observe the perfect-postured yoga masters, I'd remind myself that these judgements are a standard part of our infant practice.

Helen invited us to move from the habitual act of doing to inhabiting the body and simply being. The self-consciousness that had occupied me began to wane, to be replaced, in fact, by a fleeting sense of gratitude for the modest padding I'd accrued in my posterior over the years.

She continued: 'When readiness settles, beckoning attention to the breath, one embraces the physicality of each inhalation and exhalation. The breath flows unaltered and untamed, a natural rhythm affirming perfection in the present moment and completeness embraced effortlessly, allowing the breath to be.

'In the mind's eye, let an image form of a lake, its waters cradled by the earth, an embodiment of receptivity. Whether deep or shallow, tranquil or stormy, the lake mirrors nature's dance, from serene reflections to turbulent ripples, a canvas alive with the play of light and shadow.'

I pictured my 14-year-old self perched on that familiar rock in the cove at Ladestown. Fragments of old distress surfaced, threading through my thoughts: the endless hours spent by the shoreline, watching the lake without fully understanding why it eased something in me, only knowing it did.

'The lake, a canvas of possibilities, may wear the cloak of deep indigo or shimmer with the clarity of emerald. On calm days, its surface mirrors the world above, a flawless reflection of trees, rocks and the shifting sky. But with the arrival of wind, chaos stirs, distorting the once-perfect image into a dance of ripples, catching sunlight like scattered diamonds.

'As night descends, the moon takes centre stage, casting its ethereal glow upon the water's surface, painting a picture of tranquillity amid the darkness. Even in winter's grip, when icy fingers seize the lake's surface, life persists beneath, a silent symphony of movement and vitality.'

Over the years, I've witnessed the lakes of Westmeath play the sky's reflection: not a single ripple to disturb the surface and then, in a mood swing, morphing into the raging North Atlantic, like waves crashing against Ireland's western edge. I've walked across their icy tops, feeling like Ernest Shackleton, and witnessed them flip-flop between states faster than a politician's promise.

Helen again: 'Linger here, inhaling deeply, conjuring the essence of a tranquil lake in your mind's eye, gradually integrating it within yourself until you and the lake become one. Let your awareness encompass all energies with kindness and understanding, mirroring the lake's serene embrace by the earth. Breathe as the lake breathes, feeling its essence meld with yours, your mind and heart receptive to each passing moment, reflecting clarity or turbulence alike. Embrace moments of utter calm, where surface and depths merge seamlessly, and others where ripples disrupt the mirror, obscuring reflections and depth momentarily.'

Perhaps I'd always found solace in the lakes because I recognised myself in them. On some days, I mirrored their stillness – calm, connected and at ease; on others, I felt like the churned-up waves, pulled beneath the surface by a maelstrom of upheaval. Then there were times I felt nothing at all, distant and dulled; and others when my thoughts and emotions shifted and shimmered like the ever-changing face of the water – restless, alive and fluid.

'As you sit here, merely observing the interplay of your own mental and emotional energies, the transient thoughts and feelings, impulses and reactions, ebbing and flowing like ripples and waves, take note of their influence. Just as you engage with the myriad changing energies that dance upon the lake – the wind, the waves, the light, the shadows, the reflections, the colours and the scents – notice how your thoughts and feelings affect the surface and clarity of the mind's lake. Do they stir up turbulence, clouding the waters? And is that acceptable? Isn't a rippling or wavy surface simply part of the lake's nature? Could you possibly identify with the surface and the entirety of the water body, becoming the tranquillity beneath the surface, where only gentle undulations persist, even amid choppy and rugged surface conditions? Similarly, in your meditation and daily life, can you remain attuned to the shifting content and intensity of your thoughts and feelings and the vast, unwavering reservoir of awareness itself residing beneath the surface of your mind? In this regard, the lake serves as a teacher, reminding us of the lake that lies within ourselves.'

As you watch the ever-shifting surface of Lough Ennell, Lough Owel or Lough Derravaragh, it's easy to be taken in by the movement: the ripples, the gusts, the occasional flurry of drama stirred by wind or weather. But the real substance, the true volume of life and water, lies beneath: steady, undisturbed, entirely indifferent to the surface performance. In much the same way, our lives unfold in constant flux. The days bring change, the weeks bring noise, and the years carry us through all manner of impermanence. We ride those waves, often forgetting that there is something more solid beneath all of it, something that holds steady. That's what we can learn from the lake. And whether or not you believe it today, that same steadiness lives in you, too. It doesn't vanish on the chaotic days and doesn't depend on stillness to exist. It simply waits. And as you move, little by little, towards that untainted, consistent part of yourself, you'll start to recognise it again.

Helen continued. 'In this tranquil moment, as we linger, we embody the essence of the lake in silence. Here, we affirm our capacity to embrace, without judgement, all facets of our being – mind and body, just as the earth cradles the lake, reflecting the celestial dance above – the sun, moon, stars, trees, clouds and sky. It mirrors life's beauty, stirred by the breeze, which lends it vitality and sparkle moment by moment.

'So, let us continue to immerse ourselves in the lake's meditation in quiet contemplation. Embrace the storms and moments of serenity within, as the lake does, embodying its tranquil depths amidst life's ebb and flow. Be the lake.'

I often think back to that humid summer morning in 1994 when I hopped on my battered bike without much thought. Looking back, it feels less like I chose to go there and more like I was summoned, as if the land recognised I needed its steadiness. That, to me, is the essence of spirituality. It's not tied to religion, institutions or doctrines; it's rooted in the unseen threads that bind us – to the earth beneath our feet, to the people who walk beside us, and to the moments that remind us we're never as alone as we think we are.

When considering wisdom, I think of those who have been around long enough to acquire it. The land, the lakes and the earth existed long before we arrived on them and will exist long after we are gone. They have witnessed all the triumphs and tribulations of evolution and civilisation. Perhaps this ancient wisdom, etched into their very existence, makes them patient and influential teachers for anyone willing to pause, listen and learn.

Every good teacher needs a willing student. And as I continue to learn from the land, I find myself drawn back, again and again, to the lakes in meditation and presence. The best teachers don't hand you answers; they point you towards your own. They guide without leading, nudge without pushing, and remind you that the path is yours to follow. That's why the lake meditation is a powerful companion. It reveals the stillness. It shows us that the surface will shift – calm one moment, turbulent the next. In time, one learns not to wage war against the storm, nor to idolise the calm, but to trust in the truth: underneath it all, there is a stillness, a centre, that does not flinch.

Rather than conquer chaos, we remember what lies below. We learn to be the lake.

Audio track

I began writing this piece in the very place where my life-long bond with the lake first took root: I returned to the same cove that, at 14, had opened its arms to me, and I sat on the same weather-smoothed rock, beneath the same trees, beside the same sandy shore. Remarkably, almost absurdly, very little had changed. The paths were worn just enough, the breeze still carried the same woodland hush, and the water still moved in that familiar, unhurried way.

It was just after ten in the morning, the same time of day as it had been back then. The only thing missing was my old bicycle, which I sincerely hope has since been melted down and reborn as something more practical, perhaps a toaster.

I set my phone down by the water's edge. I tapped 'record', hoping to catch the soundscape just as it had been in the summer of 1994: the soft lap of the lake against the shore, the murmurings of the forest, birds exchanging whatever gossip birds exchange, and that low, persistent hum of a world quietly getting on with things.

And there it was, unchanged, undramatic, utterly itself – that same steady rhythm. So much in my life had shifted in the years since I first heard it: entire versions of myself had come and gone, and yet the lake had not. It remained indifferent and beautifully unmoved by the messiness we humans insist on dragging to its edge.

Later, at home, I slipped on a pair of headphones, played the recording on a loop, and sat at my slightly weary piano, one key forever a semitone off. As the melody began to take shape, I recognised it almost immediately. It had that quality of being new and remembered, like the lake itself.

I wanted the music to hold what the lake had always taught me: that while the surface might ripple, shimmer or storm, there is always something steady beneath it. Something waiting to be heard.

The recording of the lake is woven into the piece itself: the actual sound of that morning at the cove is embedded in the music. This composition is an invitation, a guide, to visualising the lake through the lens of mindfulness meditation — to not just see it but to feel it — and to rest in its stillness, and then, as the piano opens, to embody it.

To *be* the lake.

Chapter 7

Be the Mountain

From the first stroke of the sweeping Shannon to the scenic shores of Lough Allen and the cloud-crowned peaks of Carrauntoohil, the rivers and mountains that have witnessed centuries pass, nourished the land and bestowed the senses.

The paradox of beauty and peril, a parable of life's path.

Moments of pleasure and pain, content and calm waters before the storms and the rain.

From the lowest point we shall ascend, so our collective voices may echo from the summit.

But to rise, you must first awake. Acknowledge our responsibility to leave this place in a better state, to protect the vulnerable and transform their faith.

For what use is wealth, growth and prosperity when there is such disparity?

Families waiting years for some clarity, somehow a tolerance for such austerity of spirit.

We rise up for these children, not to lament the past, but to alter a future unwritten.

We rise up for their guardians, their friends, their grannies and grandads, their brothers and sisters, their aunties and uncles, their pets and teachers, their communities and their dreams.

But we also rise up for the child within, the child who never felt comfortable in their skin, the child who could not express or begin to make sense of the chaos in their mind, who sat in class and asked, 'What happened to Kurt Cobain?'

THE PLACE THAT HAS NEVER BEEN WOUNDED

Only to be met with a deafening silence of shame.

We rise up for the child within who grew up in a world that weaponised sin, lessons of numbers, languages, science and theology, celebrating conformity and denouncing autonomy.

But we invite you to rise up, too, a collective power for change, a unified voice that can't be ignored.

Do it for the youth and kin, but also do it for the child within.

The bone-tired tribe assembled in Cronin's Yard at the base of Ireland's highest peak, Carrauntoohil, in the majestic county of Kerry on the southwest coast of Ireland. It is easy to see why they call this part of the country 'the Kingdom', though depending on the weather, you wonder whether to worship or fear it.

The day was just getting started, and the Macgillycuddy's Reeks were dressed in the mist and haze of first light, as if the land was still waking and half dreaming, attempting to hide behind the mask of dawn. In a bid to scrape together whatever scraps of energy I had left, I stumbled into the little tea-room café nearby and grabbed a can of Coke – my salvation in caffeine and sugar. Of course, the local wasps, drunk on an unexpected stretch of Indian summer, decided they wanted a sip, too, and promptly placed me under siege.

In a display of Darwinian bravado, one particularly enthusiastic zealot jabbed me right in the neck. The sting was efficient and ruthless, as if to say, *You've been warned.* Of course, there had been warnings – plenty of sage advice about the harmlessness of these striped drifters: 'Ah, they're only minding their own business!' and 'They won't bother you if you don't bother them!'

Well, that little prick proved us all wrong, literally. The sting flared up, a sharp little reminder of nature's indifference. Luckily,

I had a makeshift pharmacy tucked into my hiking bag, complete with a couple of antihistamines, to keep my day from completely derailing. An interesting start, as I popped the pill: 'May cause drowsiness.' *Wonderful.*

We were taking part in 'The Rising' – the challenge we were now knee-deep in. The Rising wasn't just a physical and mental feat; it was a way to channel something deeply personal into something tangible, to raise funds for a cause close to my heart – the charity I co-founded, A Lust for Life, with my close friends Paula and Colm. Our charity has a singular mission: to build and expand evidence-based early prevention mental health programmes for children. We want to give kids the tools to be more effective guardians of their minds and emotional well-being, skills that many of us never had the chance to learn until life had already kicked us around. At the time of writing, we're reaching nearly half of all Irish primary schools and are determined to be in every school nationwide within the next two years. Our programmes aim to teach children that all emotions – joy, sadness, anger and fear – have a place and a purpose, guiding us through this winding path we call life. Because let's be honest: life doesn't follow a tidy, linear path. It's a journey filled with peaks and valleys, moments of suffering, pleasure, pain, love and exhilaration.

Over the past six days, this group of extraordinary humans had hurled themselves headfirst into a savage test of endurance. We'd kayaked the entire stretch of Ireland's longest river, the mighty, meandering Shannon; wrestled with three of its biggest and most brutally temperamental lakes, Loughs Allen, Ree and Derg; then cycled 170 unforgiving kilometres along mountain roads and through weather that could only be described as biblical. And, somehow, we'd made it here, to the base of Ireland's highest peak.

What began as a physical challenge had quickly become a test of emotion, spirit and vulnerability. Things that week came to the surface for many of us, truths we'd hardly dared to face. Fatigue and pain peeled back the layers, revealing an exposed edge rarely shown. Yet, there was a strange comfort in it – a safety in knowing that every crack and fragment of ourselves was welcome in this group. On those long, energy-sapping days, nothing was off the table. Apart from my neck, apparently.

Getting to the start line had taken no small amount of training: the kind that consumes your evenings, your weekends, and a fair bit of your sanity. And somewhere in all that sweat, repetition, sunburn and capsizing, a moment captured the essence of why we were doing this. A moment so finely etched, so oddly resolute, that I suspect it'll be among the final few to flicker when the lights begin to dim on my life's journey. We were at the business end of a long, punishing paddle along the River Inny as it wound its way through the heart of County Westmeath. Those days were tough, each blending into the next, our minds dulled by the endless, isolated hours on the water. We might go five or six hours without seeing another soul; with each bridge, we passed a lonely arch of stone under which we would drift, hoping for even a passing stranger to wave to or share a few words about the reliably miserable Irish weather.

As we approached a low, weathered bridge now, Paul Boyce, an old school friend and, without fuss or fanfare, one of the most remarkable men I've ever known, came to an abrupt halt against the will of a restless current. At first I thought he might need a sip of water or a breather. But then it became evident it was something far heavier than fatigue. Ray Carolan, a good friend and the steady hand guiding our challenge, drifted over without fuss. In a low voice, he explained that this was the bridge where Paul's mother had taken her life not so long ago. My mind went blank, stunned by the weight of what Ray had said. I slowly paddled up beside Paul, who sat motionless in his kayak. I didn't say a word; I just stayed there beside him, close enough to let him feel I was there, ready to go through it with him; that we could pass under this bridge together, shoulder to shoulder. In that still moment of grief, of shared strength, I felt the depths of what it means to be there for someone, not needing to fix or intervene, but to honour their space without judgement.

Paul finally broke the silence with a small, grateful smile and remarkable yet trademark warmth. 'Thank you, lads,' he said, gently. 'I'm all right. Let's keep rolling.' And so, we paddled forward. Going under that bridge that afternoon was one of those ordinary moments with extraordinary consequences. It was a stark reminder of an Ireland shaped by quiet, unspoken sorrows, of a time when pain and shame kept too many from facing another day. But as we pushed on, I felt a shift in all of us: a shared resolve to build a community where no one would have to bear such things alone, where we would leave those shadows behind for good.

It's experiences like these that forge unbreakable bonds within a group. Bonds that aren't born from motivational speeches or nights out fuelled by beer, kebabs and drunken bluster. They're ingrained, rooted on a cellular level, souls in sync. One thing I've learned in my work is that to take on the truly remarkable challenges in life, you need a remarkable team. Individuals can accomplish a great deal, but a group's collective energy makes the hard work feel a little lighter. And that bond? We would lean on it repeatedly during our challenge's long, relentless days.

There were plenty of harrowing moments on the wrathful waters of Lough Ree and Lough Allen. My deep-seated primal fear of getting trapped under a capsizing kayak in rough weather was never far from my thoughts. Sleep was a luxury that week, too, and I was missing my partner, family and dog, Stevie. They lingered in the part of my mind that wasn't hijacked by unease.

After a gruelling 170-kilometre cycle, facing the worst that the Wild Atlantic Way could throw at us, I knew there was a punishing climb on the bike to the base of Carrauntoohil. I didn't mention it to the others: I could see they'd hit a wall. I was one of the most experienced cyclists, so was just about managing, but this was always about the group, not just making it through individually.

As soon as the gradient began to rise, I watched the guys' heads drop. The wind whipped in from the side and a brutal gale turned the climb into a battle to even stay on the bike. Rain lashed from multiple angles. Paul, who'd taken a nasty fall earlier, was cut and bloodied, his shirt torn, his legs shaking. He was in the eye of the storm. This guy wasn't giving up. John and I rode up beside him, flanking him, each with an arm around his back. We told him he was getting up that climb, that we weren't leaving his side until he reached the top. Paul was in a bad place. But what I saw that day was beyond anything I'd witnessed in sports, music or any other pursuit. This climb was pure grit, a dogfight.

Paul and I were both in tears as we pedalled forward. I whispered to him that his parents would be proud. His father had passed away a year before the Rising challenge from cancer, but I could feel them there, right alongside us. And so we climbed, honouring the ones who believed in us and those who weren't with us any more, at least not in person.

We collapsed off the bikes at the summit, unravelling and releasing the repressed grief and unsaid stories like an elastic band pulled back and catapulted away. The rain had soaked us through, leaching into our bones.

The harsh and unrelenting wind tore through the car park, scattering our families and friends like leaves caught in a storm.

In that huddled embrace, words were useless: only we, this small, exhausted group, could grasp the enormity of what we'd endured. Louize and my family were weeping as I stumbled into their arms. My nephew Billy wrapped himself around me, his hug fierce and unwavering, as if willing his strength into my exhausted frame.

In his grip, I felt something else that felt unbreakable. We were doing this so that his generation and those who follow wouldn't grow up in the same society that Paul's mother and many others had endured.

Yet, despite the relief of that embrace, I knew this journey wasn't over. Ahead of us loomed another challenge, a final ascent, a high peak crowning the entire country: Ireland's highest summit, Carrauntoohil.

I've always had a strange fascination with mountains. Which is odd, considering I grew up in the Midlands of Ireland, where the closest thing we have to elevation is the occasional bumpy esker or the odd drumlin: a thank-you to the glaciers who, thousands of years ago, did their best to give us something to look at. But let's be honest: if something rises above knee-height in Mullingar, we call it a hill and give it a name.

When we were kids, my parents would throw us all in the car and drive up to Donegal, my dad's homeland, for our summer holidays. These trips were always barely contained mayhem: four or five kids packed into the backseat of a Volkswagen Jetta, all on regular and uncoordinated pee schedules. But one sight on these trips never failed to silence us – a rare miracle – which was the first glimpse of Benbulben rising from W. B. Yeats Country, weather-worn, brow furrowed like a poet mid-verse.

Usually, the car was a cacophony of whinging and unclaimed flatulence. But as we drove under the looming shadow of

THE PLACE THAT HAS NEVER BEEN WOUNDED

Benbulben, the vehicle would go deathly quiet, like some divine hush. It was massive, raw, almost unnatural, as if it had been designed by God to shut kids up on long journeys and give the parents a reprieve from their irritating offspring. And it worked. Benbulben was a mountain that demanded attention, even from a gang of half-feral children full of Fanta and Skittles, strapped into a hatchback.

Whenever mountains came up in geography class or I heard tales of far-off peaks, my mind would always wander back to Benbulben. It didn't matter if we were poring over the Alps, the Andes or any other range in the textbook – I'd find myself picturing that unmistakable shape, rising quietly from Yeats Country, as though it were the only mountain worth imagining.

Mountains have always held a specific symbolism for me – an unyielding, unmoving power that dominates the skyline. Something about a mountain's constancy and permanence rings with meaning. Growing up where I did, as I said, mountains weren't exactly on the local tour, so when I observed them, it was as if the landscape was teaching me a lesson in resolve, a strength that doesn't waver or need an audience – not unlike the lessons learned by the lake. It's a force that doesn't seek attention, doesn't care if you're watching, and yet commands respect simply by its existence. For someone who spent their early years surrounded by open fields and gentle hills, that grandeur is inescapably noticeable: a reminder of the power in standing still, of being a landmark in an unceasingly fluid world.

The Rising challenge was meant to embody life's journey. Like life, it would be a mix of stunning and joyous stretches: times when we'd find ourselves in awe of the beauty surrounding us; and other times, when it'd be dark, brutal, dull and physically demanding. And then, of course, those rare moments that change something in you that you carry forward long after. The challenge wasn't just about raising funds; it was a living metaphor for the reality that Paul and all of us know so well: life can be beautiful but also heartbreakingly brutal. And it's in accepting that contrast and embracing the highs and the lows, the tedious stretches and the transformative moments, that we learn to keep going and rising.

Finishing this challenge with a mountain, specifically the highest mountain on the island, felt fitting. I'd imagined this moment for years and visualised it down to the last step. Something about Ireland's wild, untamed beauty makes it the perfect metaphor for resilience, endurance, and everything life throws at us. Standing on a summit that's seen it all, waving the A Lust for Life flag, silently witnessing our long, tangled history from the best seat in the house, would feel like the only fitting end. There would be power in looking out over the land that had held all our triumphs, losses and everything in between. Ireland laid bare, her summits and lowlands reminding us of our own.

After dispatching a wasp that seemed to think my neck was its personal enemy, we set our sights on the mountain. Having my sisters, Julie and Andrea, and my brother-in-law, Malcolm, along made it all the more memorable. The day was unexpectedly mild, but a faint sense of unease lingered – the sky kept us guessing. Some clouds had taken on a distinctly menacing hue, and after enough uninvited downpours on mountains, I knew better than to take a promising start at face value.

The climb would begin with a 5 km trek up to the Devil's Ladder, the steepest stretch of the ascent. But first we had to get there. Conversations buzzed around us as we walked, voices blending with the sounds of heavy footsteps and breathless bodies, but I found myself retreating into silence. I had a lot churning in my head, and flashbacks of my life's journey surfaced along the way. These weren't painful memories but legacies from darker times, reminders of where I'd been and where I stood now. Above all, however, I felt a deep pride in the people around me and, surprisingly, myself. And as we reached the base of the Devil's Ladder, something unexpected happened. The thick mist that had wrapped itself around the mountain began to lift. Shafts of sunlight broke through the clouds, glinting off the lakes and waterfalls as if nature were rooting for us. One of the guides mentioned that if the sun stayed out, we were in for quite a view at the summit. With each step towards the top, the clouds and mist continued to peel away, and by the time we'd conquered the Ladder, ready for the final push, we were shedding jumpers and standing in T-shirts. Nature was cheerleading us to the summit.

A hush fell over the group as we made the final push towards the peak. We'd hit the Carrauntoohil jackpot: blue skies stretched endlessly around us, wrapping the summit in an impossibly clear view. From up here, you could see right across to Dingle and the Atlantic Ocean, the land rolling onwards as far as the eye could see.

Only at the top did we start to grasp the true expanse of these mountains, their jagged, raw beauty laid out like something that will stand forever. At that moment, I thought about everything these mountains endure, but also everything they have witnessed. The surface shifts and weathers, but the mountains remain, rooted deep into the earth, stitched into the very crust of the island. They're imposing but somehow welcoming, breathtakingly beautiful, yet carrying a subtle threat that demands your respect.

Reaching the summit, I found myself once again beside Paul. We stood there in stillness, soaking in the vastness around us, the humbling beauty of it all. I turned to him and, in a quiet voice, I muttered John Muir's words: 'You are not in the mountains; the mountains are in you.' These mountains had become part of us, carved into our bones as much as they were etched into the land.

My live show, for all its supposed pressures, is oddly comforting. A space where thoughts assume a supporting role. Over time, I've realised that if you prepare with discipline and blind faith, the stage stops being a trial and starts being a well-earned victory lap: a wink to all the unseen hours behind the curtain.

The show had a flow: music, spoken word, guests, monologues. I loved performing it. The audience never knew what to expect. My favourite part? Spotting the awkward partner, clearly dragged along with the promise of pints after I'd finished banging on about mental health and depression. Arms folded, eyes darting to the exit, while occasionally shuffling to wake up their arse that had fallen asleep.

The irony? They were always the ones who got the most from it. The ones who came in sceptical and left, if not enlightened, pushing open a door they hadn't even realised was locked.

Refining the show is key. Take the feedback and tweak what needs tweaking, but don't let yourself drown in analysis paralysis. Pick it apart, sure, but don't let it pick you apart. There was one particular section, though, that, no matter how many times I performed it, sent my mind into a late-night post-show spiral. Racing thoughts, rewinding, replaying, rewording. Should I have said it differently? Should I have said it at all? I wasn't happy with it, and it was beginning to be a problem for me.

I had also become increasingly uncomfortable with standing on stage, pontificating about a life best lived. As if I had it all figured out. As if I weren't just as tangled in the mess of it as everyone else. Sometimes, it felt like playing a character. There is pressure to deliver *answers* and tie things up in a BuzzFeed-friendly 'Top Five Ways to Beat Anxiety' list. It is as if something so complex, so profoundly human, could be condensed into a handful of easy steps. I couldn't do it any more. Not like that. Because real life doesn't fit into bullet points, nor does real change.

I was heading up the N4 to do a show in Sligo in northwest Ireland and, as I had as a child, I was looking forward to my first glimpse of Benbulben. It owns the landscape. A mountain with the power to hijack your attention completely. I had to pull in. Stop. Stare. It has that gravitational pull on awareness.

That night, I had planned, as always, to wrap up the first half of the show with that troublesome, carefully rehearsed monologue. A polished, well-crafted piece that tied everything up in a neat little bow. But in the shadow of that mountain earlier in the day, watching it loom over Sligo as it had for centuries, I decided to approach the show differently.

I scrapped the monologue. Instead, I admitted the truth. But rather than leave it there, I framed it in a way that put the power back in the audience's hands. I spoke of Benbulben, of how it had watched over Sligo for centuries, unchanged, unshaken, a steadfast custodian of the land, unshaken by time.

The energy in the room altered. Subtle but undeniable. Shoulders loosened, breaths deepened. Maybe they weren't broken. Perhaps they didn't need fixing or saving. Maybe they were already doing the most challenging thing of all. *Showing up. Holding on. Getting through.* And perhaps, that was enough. While every guru and influencer peddled the idea that people were missing something, needed fixing, needed *more,* the truth was that they had already been through the fire and come out the other side.

It felt *right*. It felt *honest*. And, in truth, far more impactful than any pre-packaged life lesson ever could be.

As we walk this path towards the place that has never been wounded, we must do more than observe the land. We must learn from it. Because the landscape holds lessons. In its stillness, its endurance, its defiance against the elements.

Whatever your Benbulben is, we learn to *be* the mountain.

Audio track

The music and practice accompanying this chapter was crafted with an intention: to embody the constant, steady power of a mountain, unfolding like a story told in whispers. I wanted each note and pause to reveal itself gradually, like mist lifting from a mountainside, slowly exposing the panoramic vastness and solidity beneath.

It begins gently, an understated entrance, building with time to echo a strength that rises within, inviting the listener to find that same enduring mountain inside themselves. Striking that balance between empowerment and calm is a delicate task. Lean too far into either, and the heart of it slips away. This music will create a moment of clarity and be a mirror that shows us what we may not always see: that no matter what the storms life have sent our way, we remain unchanged and unbroken.

The piano melody is melancholy, yet optimism is layered throughout the movement. I imagined myself as a child again, gazing up at Benbulben, wordless, held by its vastness. Just as I once looked at Paul, watching him reach the summit of Carrauntoohil, a figure against the wild sky

THE PLACE THAT HAS NEVER BEEN WOUNDED

embodying that calm, steady strength that words don't quite do justice.

This piece offers a path, a soundtrack for stepping closer to that untouched place within us, that part of ourselves that has never been wounded, from where we can draw our quiet strength.

Chapter 8

Be the Sky

The MC's triumphant voice thundering from the PA system, a booming proclamation – 'You are an Ironman!' – that echoed through my battle-worn bones, sounded like some benevolent deity delivering a final benediction. The refrain washed over me, mingling with the fading roar of the crowd as I dragged myself across the finish line, every muscle, every bone, every inch of the body and mind pushed beyond reason.

Copenhagen's city centre pulsed with a feverish, electric energy. Well-wishers, families, friends, all packed in tight, their faces turned towards the finish line, washed in the hazy glow of the hot summer sun. They came to cheer, to witness the madness that gripped their loved ones, urging us on towards a goal few understood but all somehow respected. A 3.9 km open-water swim, a 180 km cycle and a marathon for dessert.

What can I say? My mid-life crisis came prematurely. In 2016, to be specific.

My legs buckled while my body rebelled, surrendering to gravity and lactic acid as I collapsed onto the sweat-stained cobbled streets. I had imagined this moment countless times, picturing myself running across that line with defiant fists raised, wrapped in the tricolour Irish flag. But there is no way to train for this feeling – the pain, the relief, the tidal wave of emotion that crashes into you when it's finally over. The ferocity of it leaves you exposed, stripped bare. A volunteer rushed over, a thin, wiry chap with a look of practised yet genuine empathy, but as he tried to yank me up, my 17-stone frame took him down with me. A team of volunteers clustered around, hoisting my battered remains up like a group of friends trying to steady a drunken mate outside a nightclub. For a second, I half expected a soggy kebab to materialise in my hand.

As I swayed, my eyes scanned the crowd, searching through the blur of sunburnt faces until I found them – my family. They were pushing forward, elbows out, eyes fixed on me, fighting their way to the front of the barriers. A surge of emotion broke through as I stumbled towards those I love most with my last scrap of moxie. And then I was in their arms – my mother's familiar warmth, my father's unbreakable grip of pride. I clung to them, all stoicism melting away, sobbing uncontrollably, anchoring me in place as the world spun.

They had no idea what I had just been through over the previous 36 hours. But in that moment, none of it mattered. At that moment, I was simply a brother and a son, safe, held, loved and profoundly grateful.

The past few days had been some of the darkest I could recall – a haze that completely eclipsed everything else, leaving a time-worn emptiness in its wake. What made it all so unbearable was the wishful assumption I'd hopefully held on to over the last few years: that my shadow self had finally vanished, exorcised. I'd thought those deep waves of despair were destined to stay in the past, filed away as remnants of a fragmented and fractured spirit. And yet, here they were again, creeping back.

The irony stung. The last time I'd felt a mind riot such as this, I'd been in this very city, here to support friends taking on the Ironman. That unwelcome afterglow burnt the skin, sharp and unforgiving, dragging up something ragged and dormant – a version of myself I thought I'd left for dead called back from the dark like a ghost I'd never truly laid to rest.

BE THE SKY

My training partner, Jarlath, and I had flown into Copenhagen a few days earlier to settle in and prepare. I welcomed the customary electricity of pre-race jitters; that tension was a comfort in itself, a sign of commitment and discipline. But beneath it, a buried unease surged – a dread that grew with each pendulum swing. A wave was building, gaining momentum, and I was bracing myself, not knowing if I'd break through it . . . or be pulled under.

Checking into the hotel, I was grappling with nausea that I was optimistically blaming on an overpriced chicken and stuffing sandwich disguised as food, thrown at me on the Ryanair flight over. But this queasiness had taken root in some deeper, darker place, mingling with a clammy, feverish sweat that led the receptionist to ask me if I wanted a bottle of water. The room's air conditioning wasn't a relief, either; it swung erratically between 'polar expedition' and 'oven left on overnight', as if the thermostat had its own mood swings. It was like the room was in on some private joke, keeping me in this odd dance of chills and sweats, as though testing just how many climates I could endure while requiring a PhD in electronic engineering to figure out how to use the damn thing.

As I carefully unpacked my bags, ticking off each piece of gear with methodical precision, the room walls appeared to inch closer, pressing in, the air thickening as if drawn out by some invisible vacuum. My chest tightened, and before I knew it, I was sinking onto the bed, gripped by a sudden, raw panic – a rogue wave stealing the ground from under me, leaving me gasping in a space that felt smaller and heavier with every breath.

I'd been warned this could happen before races: the 'maverick mind', as some like to call it, can turn and transform from ally to adversary in a single breath. But when you've already battled these mental ambushes in the past, they're harder to contain. They can magnify and spiral before you have had a chance to tame them. I often liken them to wildfires – how a single spark, a fleeting flicker, can ignite an entire mountain into an unstoppable inferno within moments. One thought, one tiny ember of doubt, and suddenly everything's ablaze, spreading beyond control, consuming every steady thing in its path.

I attempted to regain control and dampen the flames, but frenzied, intrusive thoughts became the wind that spread the fire. In desperation, I jumped into a cold shower, hoping the shock would suppress these feelings. It only served to enrage them. I was supposed to go down to register for the race that afternoon, but right then, the room felt like a prison – one I had no desire to leave.

I had no choice but to sit with the chaos and wrestle those thoughts into something I could understand, or at least tolerate. Lying on the floor with my legs propped up against the wall – a strange habit that always seems to calm me – I tried to slow the torrent of thoughts, to grab even a fragment of coherence from the relentless stream. But there was one thought, one image, that kept coming back, stoking the wildfire: a recurring nightmare I'd had of drowning in the Ironman swim. I saw my mother and father on the shoreline, reaching out, helpless, as I slipped under, my body sinking under the waves. That vision had lodged deep, coiling in the inky corners of my subconsciousness, feeding this draining dread. It was the root, the fuel, the flame.

All my life, I've carried this visceral, bone-deep fear of drowning. As a kid, I kept my distance from open water, even though I grew up in a town cradled by the most breathtaking lakes. They held a menace, a depth that hinted at something far darker. When I was twelve, I nearly drowned in a swimming pool. It was in Lebanon, where we were living at the time, and it happened in the deep end, where my sister Andrea was struggling to stay afloat. She'd drifted too far and, instinctively, I went to her, hoisting her onto my back to keep her above water. I remember the thrashing, the confusion, the sheer terror as we sank, tangled together, both of us out of our depth in every sense. Onlookers stood by, unsure whether we were just kids rough-housing in the water or genuinely in trouble. Thankfully, an older man, sharp enough to see what others missed, jumped in and hauled us both out. It's hard to explain how a moment like that embeds itself in you and lingers. It doesn't fade but imprints itself into memory and physiology.

That moment was the context that enveloped my Ironman journey. During my recovery from my breakdown, part of the work – my curriculum, if you like – was to confront the things that terrified me, to inch closer to the edges I'd always kept well away from. Facing down my crippling fear of water was part of this twisted syllabus.

For years, the idea of triathlon made me recoil because I'd have to swim in open water, a place I'd spent a lifetime avoiding. And if I'm honest, there's another irrational layer to this: my phobia of fish. They're relics that should've vanished with the dinosaurs. They're miserable, slippery creatures, rank-smelling, dreadful-tasting, and always, without fail, utterly depressed-looking. Have you ever seen a fish that didn't look like it was counting down the days? And don't mention *Finding Nemo* – it's a cartoon. In real life, fish are tragic little spectres of evolution that probably regret getting out of bed every day. See, I told you it was irrational.

At the root of these phobias, I suppose, was that primal, utterly rational fear of death that we all drag around with us; that icy terror – the one that grips you at odd hours and that makes your mind dance around the edges of the unimaginable. I've always been preoccupied with the idea of death, but it's not just the end itself that haunts me; it's the brutal thought of not getting to say goodbye to the people I love, of leaving too soon or having them leave me without warning.

That fear planted itself early. When I was a kid, my father would go overseas with the Irish Defence Forces and the United Nations on tours of duty and, every night, without fail, I'd dream that he'd be killed and that I'd never see him again. I carried this weight in silence, knowing better than to lay it at my mother's feet. She was already balancing a mountain, raising five of us alone whenever he was gone. As a child, I didn't have the words – or maybe the courage – to talk about it, to admit just how much that fear consumed me, waiting for a phone call or a knock at the door that Dad was never coming home.

I've always been one to think too deeply, to get lost in thoughts that most people let drift by. And it wasn't just my own mind I was entangled in; I was constantly consumed by empathy and a relentless worry for others that gnawed at me day and night. Even now, I still carry that part of myself. It's part of me that I've learned to respect, manage and value. But back then, it was like carrying a weight too heavy for one person – a relentless burden that often felt impossible to bear. The thing about it is that most Irish souls are wired this way. We're haunted by the fear of unloading our pain onto others, so we choke it down and bury it in the soft, dark earth of ourselves. We've mastered the art of turning away, numbing, coating old wounds with a laugh, a pint or a dismissive wave, as though the hurt was just an inconvenience. And so we go on, smiling with practised, conditioned ease, while the unsaid gathers like silt at the bottom of a river, thickening with each year.

Lying on the floor of my hotel room, the internal noise was a howling, unhinged symphony, each thought colliding with the next, thrashing and relentless. My phone wouldn't stop ringing – my family had just landed. 'Niall, answer your bloody phone!' Meanwhile, Jarlath was in the lobby, expecting me to come down so we could register, his patience thinning by the minute. But here I was, on the verge of pulling out, booking a ticket home, retreating from this madness altogether. And then the familiar throb crept in: a cluster headache, burrowing behind my right eye with all the subtlety of a fart in Mass. It had a way of arriving precisely at times like these, like that pain-in-the-arse neighbour who only knocks when you're already at your limit, needing nothing but insisting on staying.

Somehow I changed from my sweat-soaked clothes, threw on a fresh shirt, and headed to the lobby. I've always been good in a crisis: able to play the part and shite-talk my way through the nerves like a used-car salesman selling a banger.

We needed to get a taxi out to register, the city buzzing with athletes who seemed almost too ready, their minds steeled for the challenge of a lifetime. Once we had registered, Jarlath suggested we take a bus out to Amager Beach, to the starting point of the swim. I flinched, my mind instinctively edging towards the nearest escape. I considered feigning a last-minute emergency. Instead, I went along, forcing myself not to betray the fact that the very idea of stepping into that water made me want to turn around, jump on the next plane and vanish. The conversation drifted to the idea of a practice swim when we got to the beach. I forced a grin, nodding along. Over the past week, my calf muscles had been seizing up, causing sudden, knife-like cramps that seemed omnipresent. They call it 'phantom' pains in endurance sports – the mind playing cruel games, planting doubt right when you need courage.

I looked out over the vastness of the swim course, buoys bobbing in the distance, stretching endlessly. I couldn't shake the feeling that I was looking at my own limits, that there was no way I'd get through it without slipping under. At that moment, I made the decision.

I wasn't doing the Ironman.

THE PLACE THAT HAS NEVER BEEN WOUNDED

I told my family that I needed time alone to focus and get my head in the right place for the big day. How could I tell them I was thinking of throwing it all away after they'd gone to such trouble and expense to be here, to watch me cross that line? And Jarlath – how could I let him down? This man had sweated and suffered alongside me, day after day. I owed him more than a vanishing act.

Sitting in my room, trying to choke down a pizza that tasted like cardboard and regret, I talked to my grandfather, Bumper. A few psychics have told me over the years that he's my guardian angel, watching over me with his massive six-foot-six frame. Bumper and I were close – he was the kind of man who'd sit quietly with you and say everything without a word. Whether you believe in guardian angels or not, at that moment, I did; I had to. It gave me some strange comfort to imagine him there beside me, his presence steady, his hand on my shoulder as I wiped away tears and pizza sauce from my face.

Lying on the bed after we'd said goodbye, I knew sleep wouldn't come that night. My mind was a tangled mess of fears and doubts, a noise I couldn't drown out. So, as a last resort, I reached for my phone, scrolling through YouTube in search of anything resembling peace – meditation music, maybe something to soften the edges. As the videos played, one caught my attention – a guided visualisation.

The voice was warm and inviting, speaking of the sky, of its vastness. Sometimes, it's thick with clouds, black and weighty, pressing down; other times, the clouds scatter, drifting lazily, leaving clear, blue spaces. And then there are those rare days when it's nothing but pure depth, a blue so vast it's as though you could fall into it forever. The sky, the voice reminded me, is always shifting, always changing. Just like the thoughts, the emotions and the storms we hold inside. They come and go, darken and clear.

BE THE SKY

It felt as if I was taking my first breath in days. I closed my eyes and pictured that moment on a flight when you break through the clouds and the grey dissolves, and suddenly, you're above it all, looking out at an endless expanse of blue stretching to the horizon. It's a world untouched, a pure, boundless silence. There's clarity there, an infinity that makes everything below feel small and manageable, as if all the noise and weight could fall away, left behind in the churning clouds beneath. Just blue – open, steady and utterly endless. The intrusive thoughts of death, of drowning, of unfinished goodbyes began to lose their grip, the frequency of their cadence draining away. They drifted in like clouds, heavy, dark, but then moved on, parting to reveal that calm blue sky beyond. I could feel my heart rate settle, the pounding fade, as the wildfire of emotion that had raged within me finally began to dampen. It was as if the storm had exhausted itself, each thought losing its sting, its urgency, leaving a strange stillness in its place.

It wasn't the only thing that had exhausted itself: the previous 24 hours had rinsed me. I could feel my body letting go, and what once felt impossible was now imminent: sleep.

A few hours later, I woke to the receptionist's voice, cutting through the darkness: 'Mr Breslin, this is your wake-up call.' I never trust my phone alarm to do the job. It was 4 a.m., and the city outside was still cloaked in black. But the feeling that washed over me as I opened my eyes . . . I still struggle to put words to it. It was like stepping outside myself, an almost surreal clarity as if I was watching my body, trembling with intense, focused energy. A wave of motivated anger, sharp and distilled, rattled in my bones. I felt unbreakable. There was a profound certainty rooted so deep it was immovable – by the end of this day, I would be an Ironman. I often wonder if it was a high from surviving that dark night of the soul, how you feel after a savage flu finally breaks, and that first rush of energy floods back into your veins, making you feel half-human again. Maybe it was Bumper, somehow channelling his spirit into me. Or perhaps it was my family – each of them, without even knowing it, pouring their lifeforce into me. What I remember most was this fierce, overwhelming love for them. It felt like they were part of me. I wasn't there just for myself; I was there to represent us all, every struggle, every victory, every scar. All the roads I'd travelled, every dark and beautiful moment, had led me there. And in that instant, I felt ready, as if my entire life had come down to the starting line of the Copenhagen Ironman.

As we made our way to the start line, I knew where I stood. Mark, my coach, had said it plain: 'The only question that matters on the line is – have you done the work?' And I had. No short cuts. No pretending. Music was hammering out of the speakers, matching the thud in my chest beat for beat. Then I heard Andrea's voice, cutting cut through the noise like a knife: 'You've got this, Niall! We're so bloody proud of you!'

That cracked me open. I let the tears come, just enough – I didn't need to start dehydrating before the damn thing even began. We were standing on the edge of the sea, but it could've been the edge of the world. The fog was thick enough to touch. We couldn't see more than a few feet ahead, and people started murmuring about pulling the swim. No visibility. No bearings. I imagined veering off course, paddling halfway to Finland. And then, almost on cue, sunlight started forcing its way through. And not gently, either: it tore through the fog and hit the water, scattering flickering diamonds across the surface.

I thought: *Let me in.*

And it was hard to believe that, just the night before, I was half convinced I'd drown.

BE THE SKY

The moment I entered the water, something primal kicked in. Not panic, oddly, not even fear. Just a deep, instinctive recognition. As if my body, long before my brain could catch up, remembered how to belong in this element. The sea didn't resist me. It took me in. Cold, sharp and vast, but it didn't fight me. It welcomed me.

And the mind – god, the mind. For weeks, it had fed me dread, rehearsed disaster in vivid colour. But when I finally stepped into the very thing I feared most, it collapsed into silence. Not defeat, but complete peace. The fear had never been an enemy. It turned out to be an ally dressed in the wrong clothes.

When I came out of the sea, bleeding from a kick to the nose and streaked with jellyfish welts, I felt . . . light. I could've gone back in. Genuinely. I almost wanted to.

Onto the bike, and it was like rolling through a Cotswolds postcard. I was coasting. Content. Then came the marathon.

I won't sugarcoat it. That was grim. I'm not a runner. My legs protested as if it were their first time doing this. My feet were furious. My brain sulked. But, weirdly, I still loved it. Every aching, brutal step was soaked in meaning. Every cheer from the crowd, every fellow racer dragging themselves along beside me, it was like we were all plugged into the same invisible power source. We carried each other forward.

I crossed the line not as someone who'd conquered anything, but as someone who'd been changed. Those ten hours were something close to sacred. I don't say that lightly. I was floating through a kind of high, a deep, cellular calm – the kind of still joy you don't need to smile through. I felt lit from the inside, my family's arms my medal.

As we embark on this journey towards the unscarred place within us, the refuge untouched by life's wounds, countless thoughts will rise like clouds to steer us off course. These thoughts often carry an emotional weight, a charge that pulls us from presence and anchors us in the prisons of memory, where we wrestle with regret, pain and shame. Or they may launch us into the future, a landscape filled with shadows cast by our fears. These detours are inevitable; they are not failures but are intrinsic to our path. Each time we are drawn away, our task is to notice, to gently course-correct and guide ourselves back. This path is anything but straight – it winds, twists and loops back on itself in ways that, if traced, would resemble the joyful, chaotic scrawl of a child with a crayon. You will reach your destination, though not by the direct line of the crow. This journey is more like a winding route on an old map, where you are taken over hills, through winding country lanes, with unexpected turns that reveal new views. And even if they delay your arrival, the scenic route is worth it. This is why, in mindfulness, we look to the sky as our guide, an image as vast and changing as our own thoughts. Like clouds, these thoughts drift and dissolve, ever-shifting, part of a great, boundless expanse that does not hold them but lets them pass.

As we lean into the Polaris principles, we practise letting go, detaching from judgement, surrendering to the moment, and approaching each thought with curiosity and grace. Some days, the sky within will be grey, thick with clouds; other days, scattered with light, spacious with possibility; and in rare moments, a pure, cloudless blue. We are learning to witness this inner weather, to know that all states pass and that beneath it all, the sky remains.

One of the most enduring refrains in mindfulness, repeated across traditions and teachers, is this: *You are not your thoughts.* At first, it may sound abstract, even disorienting. But over time, it becomes true. We begin to see that our thoughts are not instructions, nor definitions of who we are. They are mental events, temporary, often chaotic, that pass through the mind like weather across a vast sky. The practice is not to eliminate them, but to learn to observe them. To allow them their wildness, their noise, even their darkness, without merging with them. This is the art of detaching from thoughts: creating space between the self and the thought. And it is in that space that peace becomes possible. This is what Steven Hayes, the co-developer of acceptance and commitment therapy, called 'cognitive defusion' – a way of stepping back and seeing thoughts for what they really are: passing words, images and impulses, nothing more. You don't have to believe them, obey them or argue with them. You just acknowledge their presence, like clouds drifting across the sky or cars rolling by on a street. Thoughts are like weather, and weather changes.

In meditation, this process encourages clarity. We sit, we breathe and, slowly, a new way of seeing emerges. The sky metaphor is a powerful one, not as poetry, but as structure. Like the mountain and lake meditations, it calls us back to nature's steady rhythms. The sky holds storms without judgement.

When I began this practice, I found it deeply challenging. My instinct was to fight the noise, to wrestle the mind into stillness. But, over time, I learned instead to anchor myself in what the Polaris principles lead to: the unchanging centre, the part of us that remains steady, no matter the conditions.

We must learn to let thoughts arise without letting them overtake us. To notice, without following. Otherwise, we risk being pulled away from the our path. In time, with patience and care, we stop identifying with the storm. We begin to recognise that we are, and have always been, the sky.

Audio track

The composition and audio in this chapter are crafted to mirror the many moods of the sky, capturing the ebb and flow of its shifting temperament. The melody moves purposefully, designed to echo the sky's transient nature, an ever-changing canvas. It begins simply, evoking moments of clarity where everything feels bright and open. Gradually, the music unravels and deepens, bringing forth the rolling clouds and gathering storms – the dissonant notes that echo our shifting emotions, the turbulence of thoughts. Then, like a plane ascending through heavy clouds, breaking through to boundless blue, the music returns to stillness, a clarity unclouded, a moment of unyielding possibility. Here, we're reminded of the vastness beyond each storm and of the sky's enduring openness, steady even as it shifts.

The journey through sound aims to be a reminder that no matter how thick the clouds are, there's always a clear sky above, waiting to be touched.

Chapter 9

Be the Beauty

In the benign, boundless black of the Irish bog, I glimpse the wildflower, fierce and defiant, casting contrast into the cold grip of decay.

A golden plover, tucked deep in the heather, its feathers trembling against the earth. The mist pulls back like an old curtain, surrendering to the burn of the rising sun, as the world wakes, and life whispers in the dawn's first breath.

I witness the hand-cut turf, gifted by nature's past, fuelling homes where love lingers against the icy breath of a brutal Irish winter.

A father and son, bodies bent, hands calloused, ritually turning each sod. Silent but sacred, the weight of centuries in every lift.

They sit together on the edge of their labour, flasks of tea steaming in the crisp air. Their eyes scan the small plot, their piece of earth passed down from generation to generation.

An inheritance not of gold but of soil, a pride rooted deep.

Where words are few, but the silence speaks.

In that pause, I see it:

The land is not theirs.

They belong to it,

Guardians of its breath, stewards of its memory, watching over what their fathers and their fathers' fathers broke their backs to save.

And in that quiet moment, I see love.

In the turning of sod, in the ritual, in the stillness of the shared labour.

It's more than just the earth they're shaping; it's a legacy.

Where some see death and decay, let beauty reside in the shadows of the mind.
When you find the spirit absent of colour,
Where there's light, there's hope, and where there is hope, there's light,
A flicker, a flare, in the darkest of nights.
For harmony exists in that inner fight, in that cauldron of chaos,
A vacuum of serenity and silence, of presence.
In the discomfort of dissonance, a melody in a major key,
In the rebellion of peace, be the beauty.

When I hung up my boots and retired from professional rugby in 2004, I found myself grappling with an identity crisis as profound and disorienting as the one I experienced when I first stumbled into the chaotic wilderness of adolescence. Back then, I sought refuge in rebellion, channelling my restless energy into a death metal band we grandly named RAMSCAR – an acronym that, in our satanic youthful bravado, stood for 'Rise, Almighty Satan, Come And Rule.' The Christian Brothers were not fans, as you could imagine.

Luckily, I did not intend to return to my nihilistic 'Paradise Lost' days. But I was lost. You often hear of professional athletes, once they retire, finding themselves utterly adrift. Their entire sense of identity and self-worth have been so tightly woven into their sport that when it's gone, they unravel. They are not quite sure who they are any more, as if the person they once were vanished when the final whistle blew. You spend years sacrificing so much of yourself, giving up pieces of your life to reach a destination you've long dreamed of. But then, when you finally arrive, you're struck by the unsettling truth: you don't belong, or worse, you realise you're not equipped to handle what you've fought so hard to attain. In truth, as mentioned in a previous chapter, I've come to see all my injuries as my body's way of firing a warning shot, a signal I failed to heed at the time. It was as though my body was quietly breaking down, piece by piece, so my mind wouldn't have to. Fortunately, I had music as my lifeline, a safety rope when everything else felt uncertain. But if I'm being honest, I still saw it as little more than a hobby in the early days of my music career. Deep down, I carried all the cynical baggage of, 'It's not a real job,' that I'd absorbed growing up. I convinced myself I was just trying to relive a misspent youth, stuck in arrested development, clinging to the echoes of a past that never entirely stopped reverberating. So, I needed a back-up plan.

Banking certainly wasn't on the radar when I sat across from my career guidance counsellor in school. Growing up in Ireland, I often heard people say, 'Get yourself a good, stable job – like working in a bank.' And if it wasn't that, I was repeatedly nudged towards the priesthood. My devout Catholic grandmother, Nana Mac, bless her, would quietly slip me a fiver every time I hinted that I might devote my life to God. To this day, I'm surprised she hasn't returned to haunt me, demanding her money back.

What I learned rather quickly in banking was that rampant anxiety and obscene amounts of money make for an explosive combination. Numbers and I were never the best of friends to begin with. And this was during the Celtic Tiger times, a period in Irish economic history where we collectively lost our minds over wealth. I've always maintained that Irish people are not built to be rich – it doesn't suit us, unlike the money that drifts effortlessly around London or Paris. But some of my mates, who probably still owned piggy banks, suddenly fancied themselves as the next Warren Buffett, diving headfirst into overseas commercial property like seasoned investors. The cocaine cowboys would tear through the streets of our towns and cities, all swagger and disbelief, wondering how on earth they ever clawed their way out of the grit and grey of the 1980s, back when dinner was tinned ravioli, potato waffles and processed meats so questionable you wouldn't dream of giving them to a dog today. That became €50 steaks at Shanahan's washed down with spicy mezcal margaritas. The Celtic Tiger was madness.

I didn't last long, truth be told. In fact, for all practical purposes, I fired myself from the bank. I like to imagine I had the foresight to see the 2007 crash looming, so I got out while I could. And knowing my levels of anxiety and paranoia at the time, I probably would've ended up convincing myself I was responsible for the crash, too.

During this period, I was sinking into intense pockets of depression, each one deeper than the last, robbing me of any sense of peace or ease. The world lost its vibrancy; colours dulled and even the things that once sparked joy now barely flickered, as if they'd faded into the background of a life I no longer recognised. The restless energy reverberating within me had vanished, replaced by a flatline exhaustion that left me hollowed out. Even sounds seemed muted, like the world had been wrapped in a thick, suffocating blanket, dulling everything to a distant murmur. When the fog lifted, however briefly, what remained wasn't relief but fear of its return – that bubbling dread of being pulled back into the chaos, that internal anarchy that arrived without warning and left you questioning your mind all over again.

Ironically, during that period, I found myself writing some paradoxically joyful music, a bright façade that perhaps served as a smokescreen to mask the reality I was living. Most weekends, I'd drive home to see my family, maintaining just enough self-awareness to know that alcohol was something I had to avoid. A drinking session felt like an existential threat, so the city on the weekend became a battlefield best steered clear of.

BE THE BEAUTY

One Friday evening in early October, I made my usual pilgrimage to Mullingar. We were catching the final breath of summer, the day clinging to a last shred of light as a blood-red streak of sun hugged the horizon. There's a stretch of road just past Kinnegad on the M4, where miles of trees line the motorway. I remember when the road opened and those trees were still young, barely reaching above the cars. Now fully grown, they stand tall, forming a grand, natural archway leading into Westmeath, like a beautiful driveway welcoming me home. But that particular evening, what struck me wasn't just their size but their colours: five different shades of brown, red and green, all shifting and swaying in harmony, dancing with the last rays of the autumn sun. A subtle appreciation consumed me. I noticed details rather than a general view of what surrounded me. Fragments of beauty filtered through the maelstrom of cognitive distortion.

These unexpected glimpses of beauty can leave a profound mark, often catching you off guard when you need them most. I pulled onto the hard shoulder of the motorway. Cars sped past at seventy miles per hour with a rumble that shook my vehicle as they zipped past. Yet my focus was drawn elsewhere, to the row of trees extending into the distance. It felt like an eternity since I had been completely present, connected, attentive and in my body.

Although I had travelled this route many times before, I felt like I saw it for the first time, captivated by this runway of nature. The trees in their autumn attire had compelled me to stop and admire them before moving on, and I realised that even in this tormented and dark state I could still acknowledge and experience beauty. The lesson has never left me, and there were many more periods in my life that I needed to heed it.

Like most of us, I was subtly conditioned to see beauty through a particular lens. Culture shapes the standards, dictating what is labelled as beautiful, and it is a narrow view at best: beauty becomes a carefully curated aesthetic confined to specific shapes, faces and colours. It isn't something you discover for yourself; it is something you are told to recognise. Beauty is something to be desired, an object of fantasy just out of reach. It's something you chase and admire from afar, never quite real, more an idea than a tangible reality. But Buddhist teachings speak of the impermanence of desire and how much human suffering comes from craving, a close ally of desire. We become attached to having a particular experience, and the disparity between what we crave and what we attain stirs an unease within us, an incompleteness, or what the Buddha called 'the unquenchable thirst'. When our view of beauty is confined to a narrow, rigid standard shaped by a homogenous culture, we not only overlook the real beauty that surrounds us each day, but we also suffer in chasing an ideal that can never satisfy that deeper longing. The pursuit becomes hollow, leaving us thirsting for something more authentic and satisfying.

This conditioning reveals itself most sharply in our darkest moments. You convince yourself that the only way through the chaos is to cling to the attachment of conforming to society's vacuous ideals of beauty. Whether obsessing over your external appearance or measuring others by the same shallow standards, you begin to believe that fitting into this empty mould is the key to escaping the turmoil. But it's a false salvation that only deepens the disconnection between yourself and those around you. Of course, beauty is subjective, but for the longest time, I was seduced by the belief that it was some objective, universal truth. The real tragedy of that mindset was how it blinded me to the beauty surrounding me, especially in a place as breathtaking as Ireland. And I'm not just talking about nature. The moments that don't announce themselves: the unconditional love of a dog walking beside its owner and the tenderness in that love when the owner stoops to pick up their fresh mess; the way a child throws their arms around their parent in a tight embrace when they return home from work; the artistry of a building; the design of something thoughtfully crafted; the simple elegance of a piece of art; the warmth of your mother's smile when you make her laugh; or the gentle touch of your partner when you feel vulnerable. It's a band perfectly in sync on stage, a row of trees on the edge of a motorway. It's everywhere, real beauty, if you're willing to look beyond the narrow confines of what you've been told it should be.

And this matters because, when life feels like it's knocked you flat, you don't have to search too hard to find flickers of beauty around you. I know it's tough when you're feeling lost, when everything seems out of reach. But if you can hold on to those small glimmers, those little hooks of hope, they can pull you through. They remind you that even in the worst times, there's something worth seeing and feeling; and with that, you can survive anything. My close friend Marty Mulligan once told me, 'Don't see rain as depressing; see it as earth's blessing so that things can grow.' And there will be rain on this journey towards the place within you that has never been wounded. When it falls, remember Marty's words. No matter how hard or relentless rain may be, the beauty is still there, waiting. Try to see it and recognise it amidst the floods.

The poem at the start of this chapter was inspired by one of my favourite Rumi quotes: 'The ground's generosity takes in our compost and grows beauty! Try to be more like the ground.'[5] The words remind me of the peat bogs near my hometown, in the heart of Ireland's Midlands region, a phenomenon that evolved over millennia as layers of mosses and plants slowly decomposed into carbon-laden peat soil. Every footstep on the

THE PLACE THAT HAS NEVER BEEN WOUNDED

marshland sinks softly into the ground beneath it, as if nature exhales alongside you in harmony. Your surroundings are filled with moist air carrying hints of peat and heather fragrance. Shadowed ponds reflect the sky above, while vibrant wildflowers and yellow gorse add splashes of colour to the subdued scenery. An Irish bog exudes an energy that feels almost sacred; it's a spot where time appears to pause, and the earth's murmurings beckon you to tune in and sense the age-old heartbeat of the ground beneath your feet. The bog is a creation shaped by the passage of time and the gentle touch of nature. It holds within its depths both tales of beauty and rich layers of history. For centuries, bogs have been the lifeblood of rural communities, fuelling hearths and homes. Cut and dried in ancient rhythms, turf has been a staple of Irish life for over two thousand years. I spent a few summers on the bogs, having been summoned by the fathers of some of my friends to partake in the back-breaking, hand-ruining profession of stacking turf. Only to be scoffed at due to my townie softness and tendency to whinge at the soggy ham and cheese sandwich you would be fed for your break.

I used to hate the damn place. For most people, staring out at the vast stretch of a Midlands bog is like looking at a gothic novel that never quite got finished. All you see is an endless obsidian blanket of death and decay, as if the land itself gave up trying centuries ago. Honestly, it's not a picture-postcard moment. On a bleak winter's morning, an Irish bog can feel less like nature's gift and more like a scene from a Tim Burton movie – mist rolling in, everything eerily still, the kind of place where you half expect the ground to swallow you whole.

But that is only if you choose to see it that way.

Shift your perspective, and the landscape transforms, revealing a different picture. It may not offer the conventional beauty we cherish – a sun melting into the sea or a mountain range rising defiantly into the sky – yet, in its own way, it holds something just as captivating. The bog's stillness speaks of endurance; its muted colours are the residue of a life beneath the surface, unseen but ever-present. It is a beauty that doesn't demand attention but waits steadily for those willing to look closer and observe its charm.

We often notice the subtle beauty around us when we allow ourselves to be fully present and embrace stillness. It is then that the colours of a wildflower catch the eye, the soft call of a golden plover among the heather reaches our ears, and the quiet bond of a father and son working side by side to provide warmth for their family comes into focus. To truly see the beauty, we must become part of it; we must be the beauty.

Audio track

The music accompanying this chapter, 'Be the Beauty', was a piece I composed with a particular blend of melancholy and pleasure in mind. Akin to that fine line between a smile and a sigh. It is in the key of D minor, which reminds me of Nigel Tufnel's unforgettable line from the film *This Is Spinal Tap* when he suggested that D minor is the 'saddest of all keys', claiming it could 'make people weep instantly'.[6] (While I respect Nigel's impeccable ear for emotional devastation, I've always felt A minor holds the true crown for inducing brief sonic depression. But each to their own in the key of sorrow.) For me, 'Be the Beauty' was an exercise in exploring that paradox: where beauty emerges from the grey, the ordinary, and even the mundane. It's not all about bright, shiny things but about finding grace in the subtle, the understated. I wanted to capture how melancholy can wrap itself around you, soft and insistent, yet within that sadness, there's a quiet kind of joy, an unexpectedly comforting depth. I attempted to achieve that with a dynamic that slowly builds into a moment of recognition, where beauty becomes evident.

My friend and mentor, Nóirín Ní Riain, reads the spoken-word piece. She invites us to step off the juggernaut of modern life and truly see what surrounds us, even if at first glance it appears drained of colour and short on anything we'd typically consider beautiful. It offers a gentle, urgent reminder: beauty is not some distant ideal, but something quietly concealed in the corner of each moment, if only we slow down enough to notice.

Chapter 10

Be Your Truth

It's like the wind takes you, and something then controls the sail.
But the wind will still blow you where the wind wishes.
And the sea will take you and carry you where it wishes.
And sometimes you'll be like me, floating on a surface of sensuality and just absorbing everything in a chaos that you can't even put anything together in; you can't make any sense of what you're living through.
And other times, you will find yourself alone. Alone, alone, alone in the dark.
You'll find yourself lonely; you'll find yourself isolated.
And in all those different situations, the continuum is your response, your obedience, your surrender.
That when the river blows you and moves you, when the wind blows you and moves you, when life becomes chaotic, when life is going in one direction and then it takes you in an opposite direction and you don't know where you are, then in actual fact, the continuum is your response, your equanimity, your ability to say yes to whatever is happening.
And then you'll realise that the yes that you say is awakening in you the realisation that there is another presence carrying you through it.
In this whirly, burly world, there is another motherly presence holding you.
And you're in a relationship with this great mother, this great presence.
It's hard to explain it.

THE PLACE THAT HAS NEVER BEEN WOUNDED

I always remember Shams-i Tabrīzī's saying, 'Words will bring you to the door, but they cannot bring you into the house.'

Strange thing about language.

We can shape the words in a way that makes meaning and brings our consciousness to a surface of clarity.

This is what I mean. And yet everything that we say with those words, every meaning we try to shape in language, is not actually the truth.

It can bring us to the door of that truth, but entering into the space of truth is only something you can do in your heart, with your heart.

So I hope that these inadequate words are okay with you.

We'll talk again.

Michael Harding

In all its well-intentioned but wildly off-the-mark brilliance, my Facebook algorithm had clearly decided I was a soul in free fall, clinging to the edge of an existential abyss. The proof? A chaotic swirl of IQ-robbing content: stoned-looking dogs staring into the void and solemn lads earnestly turning upbeat anthems into heart-wrenching ballads of despair and heartbreak in the *Hunger Games*-like quest for virality. (When I was younger, the last thing I wanted was anything viral. Our apparently Temu-created sex education classes warned us of the potential devastation of such an outcome – 15-year-olds leaving retreats thinking their manhoods would fall off if they dared considered using them for anything other than urinating.) I've never quite grasped the appeal of taking a perfectly joyous tune and wringing it dry until it's fit only for a slow, tearful shuffle at someone's great-aunt's funeral. But there it was, an endless parade of sadness dressed as profundity. As my good friend Johnny Cronin once said, 'It's easy to write a song in a minor key.'

Lost in the mists of this foghorn of nonsense that my mind consumed daily were the Facebook inspirational pages and their millions of wellness-warrior followers like me, enchanted by the irresistible combination of transformative imagery and aspiring citations.

A sun dipping below the horizon of an ethereal lake, and the coup de grâce: an abstract quote in a frilly font plastered piously across the graphic. The kind I often stared at for a full twenty minutes, head tilted, brow furrowed, until I began to suspect it was mocking me as I could not decipher its meaning.

Then came the comments – endless, breathless comments. 'So powerful,' they declared, 'so true. I needed to hear that today.' Acres of emojis accompanied these declarations, a veritable encyclopaedia of hearts, crying faces and clapping hands that left me more puzzled than the quote itself. Was my IQ inadequate for the task of decoding this deeply moving content? Was everyone else operating on a plane of enlightened understanding I could never hope to reach?

One fateful evening, when I found myself in desperate need of a dollop of fridge-magnet philosophy, I took the plunge. Down I went, spiralling into the wellness abyss of Facebook's endless inspirational pages. I skimmed through them passively, as one might leaf through an old magazine in a dentist's waiting room, hoping that one nugget of wisdom might make sense of it all, might whisper the secrets of the universe directly into my weary soul.

And then, like a beacon through the gloom, one quote leapt off the screen. It arrested me. It commanded my attention. The image – a majestic mountain erupting from an impossibly blue sea – was accompanied by the words rendered in an ornate script: '*We only have to be lucky once; you have to be lucky every time.*'

It received a digital standing ovation. The comments were rapturous. 'So moving. Language is profoundly beautiful,' the masses proclaimed. But my mind recoiled slightly, a quiet bell of recognition tolling faintly in the distance. I knew these words. I

THE PLACE THAT HAS NEVER BEEN WOUNDED

had heard them before. Then my napping, numbed neocortex woke from its slumber. This quote was no mystical utterance from some sage atop a mountain. This was a death threat. Specifically, it was the chilling promise from the IRA to Margaret Thatcher following the Brighton bombings in 1984.

We have become so hungry, so achingly desperate for assurances that we'll be okay, for someone to tell us we're loved, that life has meaning, that our struggles will resolve into some semblance of peace, that we find enlightenment and solace in death threats from the Irish Republican Army.

Forgive my facetiousness – I was one of those folks: I craved salvation – someone to say the one thing that would alter the course of my life. Instead, I found myself face-to-face with a death threat disguised as a Facebook pep talk – the sheer audacity of it!

Our desperate hunt for meaning in the storm made me realise how tenderly human this fragile, stunning mess we call self-discovery is. I spent much of the rudderless years of my life pleading with more enlightened and ostensibly wiser individuals to provide me with a road map out of the labyrinth of loneliness and internal carnage that dictated the trajectory of my existence. I was perpetually scanning the horizon, yearning for someone to crest the hill, a saviour armed with the antidote.

I invested phantom wealth overdrafts and an inexhaustible surplus of hours into any offering, no matter how dubious, that dared to promise even a moment's mercy from the slow torment of my mind. Some of these ventures offered superficial relief. They provided a fleeting sense of control in a life otherwise devoid of it. My bookshelves, sagging under the weight of relentless hope, resembled a public library – albeit one with a singular obsession: self-help and self-discovery. I committed to online coaching courses that posited depression as an inconvenient habit easily remedied by journalling, manifesting and herbal teas. I plunged into ice baths that I did not fit in, choking on the cold while convincing myself that fortitude could be forged in frozen waters. I ingested mounds of over-priced magnesium supplements and consumed inspiring documentaries that, rather than igniting motivation, left me suffocated by the stark inadequacy of my narrative. I sat shoulder to shoulder with strangers in cavernous conference centres, watching charismatic speakers insist that the sheer force of positive thinking could banish misery. Crowds erupted in orchestrated fist bumps, gamifying the human condition until it resembled the reductionism of a clickbait article: '10 Easy Steps to Happiness'.

Each attempt, each book, course or ritual was not a lifeline but a mirage.

The wellspring of deliverance I sought was not external. And yet, it would take years to understand that the answer I craved was not waiting beyond the hill but was buried, obscured by the debris of unmet expectations, unprocessed experience, fractured self-worth, and the relentless noise of a mind too accustomed to war. And though I was thankful for the privilege of being able to explore these various well-intentioned interventions, they often left me feeling even more lost. Although a handful managed to regulate my central nervous system and tame the anxiety fleetingly, they tended to act like a plaster on a bullet wound. However, I found comfort in the camaraderie and community that often came with these initiatives, and I was grateful for that. I am also mindful that these interventions can significantly benefit others regarding life's overwhelming and challenging moments. But they failed to address the wartime, general *blitzkrieg* thoughts that battled through my mind every waking hour and sleepless night. They spoke eloquently to the cerebral, rational part of me, feeding my mind with a sense of order and purpose. Yet, they faltered when finding their way through the more elusive and even, at times, labyrinthine pathways of emotion. That guarded, ineffable realm where feelings dwell seemed impenetrable, no matter how hard I tried to convince myself otherwise. I would extol their virtues to others, constructing a narrative of progress and self-improvement, yet beneath the surface, I knew. They were skimming the surface, polishing the edges, but failing to breach the formidable, well-fortified walls of actual feeling.

Growing up, I never had much cause to interrogate these things. The Church was only too happy to dictate what we could feel and could not, its proclamations seeping effortlessly into the fabric of society and the persuasive authority of parental conditioning. Children were gently, but firmly, instructed not to be sad, not to be anxious, not to be jealous. Perfectly natural, deeply human emotions, yet we were persistently told to suppress what we already, undeniably, felt. The result was a curious dissonance – a bewildering mismatch between what we experienced inside and what we were told was acceptable to display. For young minds, it was nothing short of confusing. I was acutely aware of how much my parents were juggling, and even as a child, I didn't want to add to their burdens. So, I learned to hold my feelings at bay, packaging them neatly away in some locked, unexamined corner of my mind. But then, as I escaped the cocoon of youth and entered the high-performance world of professional sport, a new layer of conditioning emerged. We were told what to value and stand for as a team and squad – a sanitised, almost mechanical version of what it meant to belong. It wasn't a question of individuality but about conforming to an idea of collective purpose. Looking back, I see how I became an absentee landlord in my own house. The architecture of my inner life was solid and enduring, but I was rarely present to inhabit it.

There comes a crossroads in life when you are confronted by a singular, unnerving question: *What is my truth?* And in that moment, the silence can be utterly terrifying if no answer presents itself. It is like sitting in an exam, staring at a paper, clueless about what the questions even mean, let alone how they can be addressed. You begin to ruminate, spiralling backwards through the corridors of your past, feeling detached from a life lived. It's an intensely unsettling experience, this disconnect from your own story – like standing on the sidelines of your life, watching it unfold from a distance and wondering how you ended up as a spectator. In the search for clarity, for some semblance of an answer, the instinct is to reach outwards, towards guidance, inspiration or direction from others.

Believe me, I am acutely aware this could read like a 1990s rom-com where the newly dumped hero of the story stands beside the river with the city skyline as a backdrop and ponders, naively asking the universe, 'Who am I?' Or perhaps I am perilously close to seeing myself as a quotation on one of the Facebook pages I referred to at the start of this chapter . . . but there we are. I don't know how to frame it in any other way.

What is my truth?

Truth has become an unbearably loaded word. Once a bedrock of shared understanding, it has now been diluted to such an extent that we casually describe ourselves as living in a 'post-truth' society. A landscape where the delicate boundary between fiction and fact has evaporated.

Once heralded as a democratising force for knowledge, social media has transformed into an industrial-scale Dunning-Kruger research project, where those armed with the least information shout the loudest. I often liken it to that insufferable fellow one always prays not to be seated beside in a pub – the one who moans with a baroque flair about absolutely everything, scowls at joy as if it were a personal affront, and views even the most benevolent act with withering suspicion. Now imagine him not alone, but multiplied by the million, all shouting into the digital void and somehow, impossibly, being heard.

This collective erosion of truth has seeped insidiously into every facet of our culture – even into academia, where truth was once revered as the ultimate metric – standing firm above the shifting tides of personal feelings. Today, not only has truth been eroded, but it has been rendered almost irrelevant. Instead, those who advocate against it usually receive the reward, whether a world leader or a social media agent provocateur with no ideological foundation, able to twist and turn at the whim of outrage, and whether or not they are telling the truth. And so, rational, logical people are left to navigate this bizarre world with its comfort in irony – the slogan on their shirts, 'Make Orwell Fiction Again', speaks less to satire and more to the stark absurdity of our times. A grim badge of honour in a world where truth, once cherished, now feels like a legacy of a more hopeful age.

At a time when objective truth and fact have become little more than relics of the past, establishing our truth has never been more essential – identifying and defining the scaffolding upon which our lives are built. Without that solid foundation, we risk surrendering our agency to the relentless cacophony of echo chambers, each dictating what we should or shouldn't do, can or cannot say, whom we may support, and whom we must condemn. It's a disconcerting mirror of the constraints I experienced growing up in the 1980s, when church and state told us how to think, feel and act. When we forfeit our ability to construct our truth, we relinquish something far more precious than we realise: our autonomy. And if there is one lesson life has hammered home for me, it's that agency – our freedom to think, choose and live authentically – is our greatest privilege. I will never take this for granted in a country that has sacrificed so much in its fight for freedom.

Ultimately, pursuing truth became, for me, less of a chase and more of a reckoning. It wasn't some grand discovery waiting in the distance but something far more elusive, buried within. What surprised me most was how this journey didn't demand motion or outward exploration but stillness, and the courage to sit with what I had long avoided.

Mindfulness wasn't the sole solution, but a steady companion. It gave me the confidence to stay in the mess, to be present without judgement amid the noise and disarray without running from it. It taught me that truth doesn't always come as a revelation but as a slow, unearthing process. A gradual peeling back of layers, each more uncomfortable than the last. But it was in that discomfort that I found clarity. It wasn't about resolving everything at once, but about allowing myself to be open to whatever came up. Only then did I begin to see that the truth I sought was never beyond me, but within me.

But my truth was not as simple as words, language or performance. It wasn't something I could articulate neatly or display for the approval of others. My truth was an awareness and unyielding recognition of the battle I had long waged within myself. For years, what I feared most wasn't failure or loss; it was stepping away from the comfort of my mind's rational, practical and logical mechanics into the unpredictable and unkempt terrain of *feeling*. I came to realise that my truth lay somewhere between the two: leaning too heavily onto one side left me cold and disconnected, incapable of genuine connection; but surrendering entirely to the other risked leaving me untethered – a disoriented, overwhelmed wreck, unable to engage with the practicalities of life.

THE PLACE THAT HAS NEVER BEEN WOUNDED

My truth was found in balance, embracing the paradox that power and vulnerability are not opposites but partners. It was a knowing and a not-knowing, an act of surrender that required the sacrifice of ego and a relinquishing of control to make space for something greater. And in that space, I discovered my truth and a richer connection to others. Letting them into that space didn't diminish me; it helped answer questions that, for too long, had been undetermined. It helped fill the gaps that inspirational quotes, self-help books and cold showers didn't quite manage.

And this began to manifest in my life. I remember the precise moment I became consciously aware of it. I had been in a relationship with Louize for about six months – a relationship that felt real, grounding and terrifying all at once. And then, as things naturally began to deepen, I felt it: the familiar, suffocating life trap stirring inside me. The same trap repeatedly sprung when things got serious, when commitment stopped being an abstract notion and started to take form. My instinct was almost clockwork, the pattern was so predictable. When intimacy edged closer, I ran. I'd break away and retreat to the safety of solitude, heading for the metaphorical hills. Opening up that feeling part of me, the messy, vulnerable side, felt impossible. My logical, rational voice insisted that the best course of action – the *safe* course of action – was to get out of Dodge. So, I did what I'd always done: I told Louize we needed a break, spinning the well-worn excuse of 'a few months apart to figure things out'. That old chestnut. It rarely works, yet somehow, it never fails to buy you an exit. But Louize, a psychologist by profession and an uncanny reader of people by nature, didn't take the bait. She didn't flinch, fight or argue. Instead, she looked at me with assured conviction and said, 'I see you, I feel you, and I'm not going anywhere.'

At that moment, something inside me cracked open. Louize knew – she *knew* – that I wasn't running because I wanted to. I was running because it was all I'd ever known how to do. And, somehow, she could see me through all the layers of fear and avoidance. She saw my truth, raw and unguarded. And in her seeing me, I saw it too.

We are, I believe, the sum of all our life experiences – the joys and the sorrows, the triumphs and the disasters, the heartbreaks that shatter us and the heartshakes that reshape us, the pleasures that uplift and the pains that ground us, every one of them. From the top of the tower of radiant glory and the bottom of the pit of gut-wrenching failure – all these fragments come together to make the whole. This is why there is tremendous value in seeking counsel and leaning into the interventions and systems of support that come our way. The intense work begins when we look inside. The answers, healing and evolution are all in the silent, messy internal spaces. There, we find out what we stand for, and our meaning.

When I take to the stage during my live shows, I don't stand there as some oracle, handing down prescriptions for a life well-lived. How could I? I have no context for the lives my audience have lived, no understanding of the burdens they carry or the dreams they harbour. Who am I to presume authority over their stories? Instead, I offer an invitation for the audience members to seek their truth, to find the courage to turn inwards, even when it feels like stepping into a storm, to sit with the messiness, the discomfort, and the questions that have no immediate answers, and to do so with patience, non-judgement and grace. I extend this invitation to you.

The Buddha encouraged *ehipassiko* ('come and see for yourself'), inviting individuals to test his teachings against their own experience rather than relying on faith or dogma. I am not prescribing remedies, but I am giving you the ingredients to create them yourselves. We must learn to uncover our truths as we journey closer to the place that has never been wounded.

THE PLACE THAT HAS NEVER BEEN WOUNDED

Not the truths handed to us by others – those we've been conditioned to adopt by flashy marketing or IRA death threats – but the truths that live within us, waiting to be discovered.

As we move into Act III, into the heart space where the intellect loosens its grip and feeling takes precedence, that truth will stand steadfast beside you. This is the space of truth – a place where authenticity resides, the world's noise fades, and you can finally meet yourself as you are.

Audio track

Michael Harding's words have long felt like the unspoken soundtrack to my inner life. I've been fortunate enough to meet and converse with some of this earth's greatest minds and hearts, but Michael possesses a rare gift – a way of cutting through the dense fog that so often clouds my mind.

Many of you, I'm sure, are already acquainted with Michael's work. For those who aren't, let me introduce you to someone I like to think of as the Irish Buddha. His wisdom doesn't announce itself with grandiosity or demand your attention. It gently sidles up to you, almost conversational, as though he's simply untangling his thoughts in real time. That's the beauty of it. There is no pretension, no sermons. Michael shares reflections that seem like they were always directed at you. The brilliance isn't in how loudly this speaks for itself but in how deeply it reaches. The timbre and tone of his voice has always provided me with such comfort, and I hope it has the same effect for you.

This reflection and set of words, in particular, seemed to articulate what I had struggled for so long to express – not just to others but to myself. His insight framed the inexpressible, offering a language that guided me to a threshold I hadn't realised I was standing before. And in translating those words into my lived experience, they became a key. They opened the door that Shams-i Tabrīzī describes – *'Words will bring you to the door, but they cannot bring you into the house'* – the door I had feared and avoided and yet yearned to pass through. They showed me the way forward and the courage to step through it.

The music too, rises, swells and carries us towards that inevitable crescendo. That moment when the elusive space of truth reveals itself. It's in that fleeting clarity, that frequency of silence, that something unknown becomes understood. It echoes his reflections, amplifying the depth of his tone and the cadence of his words as though in gentle conversation with him. Together, they draw us in, inviting us to sit beside him in intimate dialogue – conversations with the audience and himself, a merging of sound and sentiment that holds the listener delicately yet powerfully in that space of truth, where the boundaries of emotion and understanding blur into something timeless.

I invite you to listen to the audio track now, and fall into the words of Michael Harding and 'The Space of Truth'.

Act III

Metta

Defined simply, *metta* meditation (or loving-kindness meditation) is a mindfulness practice that trains the mind to cultivate warmth, compassion and goodwill. Unlike traditional focus-based meditation, metta uses silent phrases ('I wish you peace', 'I wish you health', 'I wish you happiness') to rewire emotional habits, softening self-criticism and strengthening connection with those around us. But expand the definition and you start to see why this practice is vital now, in a world where kindness has become a radical act. Where leaders of so-called free nations spew venom like it's currency, their words dripping with contempt, their rhetoric designed to fracture. And it works. That poison doesn't stay on screens or podiums; it seeps into streets, into schools, into the way we move through each other's lives. Social media stopped being just 'something we do online' years ago. Now it's the lens through we see each other, or worse, refuse to. The algorithm rewards outrage, the feed thrives on spite. And here we are, choking on the fumes of a system that tells us empathy is weakness, that connection is naivety. Elon Musk considers it Europe's flaw – this stubborn refusal to abandon each other.

Loving-kindness – 'metta' – is punk now. It's rebellion. A middle finger to the 'every person for themselves' dystopia they're selling us. It's being in the wreckage and refusing to harden. Collective metta isn't just comfort. It's power. The kind that terrifies people who profit from our despair and apathy. Don't underestimate it. Don't romanticise it, either. This isn't a platitude or passive hope. It's the work of stitching a world back together, one stubborn act of care at a time.

In Act I, we laid out the Polaris principles. They're not rules. They're not sacred texts. They're just practical ideas — steadying, guiding and occasionally useful when (inevitably) we lose our way.

Take a moment now. Remember them. Bring them into each practice — not as baggage or obligation, but as a travelling ally.

Act III follows on naturally from the space of truth we uncovered at the end of Act II. Now, we shift focus to meaning, and the people who carry it: the ones we love, and who (on a good day) love us back. Relationships aren't a feature of life; they're the infrastructure. The scaffolding. The stitching. The beating heart of our emotional survival. There's an old, dusty and lazy myth about mindfulness — as if it's some serene solo hike into your soul, untouched by the needs or noise of others. Nonsense. Real mindfulness is crowded. Messy. Human. It reminds us we're not islands but a chaos of bridges, crossings, collisions. Family. Friends. Community. Love. Loss. And without that? Life flattens. Texture vanishes. Everything turns beige. We are made of moments and a mix of what we've lived and who we've met. Every encounter leaves a trace, shaping us in ways we rarely notice but always carry. And modern life — God bless modern life. It has done a stellar job of turning relationships into Excel spreadsheets: *What's in it for me? What am I owed? What can I get out of this?*

Those questions vibrate beneath the surface, slowly starving us of real connection. We scroll past each other. A loneliness not even trying to hide any more.

But relationships, like anything human, don't hold still. They stretch. Snap. Heal. Loop back. Sometimes they drain us.

Sometimes they save us. And sometimes, they let us feel truly seen, if we're lucky. After all, one of the most urgent human things we can do is show up first for the people we love while we still can.

Act III also turns inwards, towards that strange, sometimes awkward relationship we have with ourselves. It's no fairy tale. Some days, it's hard to meet your eyes in the mirror. But it's a relationship worth repairing. You don't get to trade yourself in for a new model. If you're patient with yourself, or just stubborn enough, it becomes a journey towards acceptance. Not of the polished, PR-ready parts, but of the shadows too: the awkwardness, the things we never post, the moments we hope no one sees. As Granny Mac used to say, with the kind of honesty only age bothers with: 'We are who we are.'

And in a culture drunk on self-improvement, constantly tweaking, fixing, optimising every last corner of the self, maybe the most radical act is this:

Stop.

Stop fiddling. Stop apologising. Just be. Sit there, in the glorious, chaotic sprawl of who you already are and know that it is, somehow, enough. Meditation doesn't make any of that tidier. But it helps us stay with it. All of it. The beautiful and the unbearable. The silence and the noise. No flinching. No edits. Just presence.

And that presence? It matters. Because impermanence rarely sends a warning. It just shows up.

That's not to say you shouldn't drive forward, set goals, chase dreams and map your ambitions with the enthusiasm of a cartographer discovering new lands. By all means, build. Strive. Aim. But don't let it become the totality of your being. Life isn't a finish line to cross, it's what's unfolding right now, in the margins and pauses. Live the life in front of you, rather than chasing one that's always just out of reach.

THE PLACE THAT HAS NEVER BEEN WOUNDED

This act and the *metta* practice it introduces also turn us outwards. They invite us to offer our love, compassion and better energy to a world desperately in need of it. Because let's be honest: the world feels broken. For many, it *is* broken. War, genocide, climate collapse, corruption that seems almost proud of itself – so much of it is beyond our control, and yet all of it weighs on the heart.

In the relatively short time I've spent on the planet, I have watched humanity bend and break, rise and roar, heal and hope. I have witnessed the Cold War melt into history, only to see new tensions rise to sate the unquenchable thirst of hyper-capitalism. I have seen real wars, not just on television screens or headlines, but in the weary eyes of those displaced and disillusioned. Genocides too horrific to comprehend. Acts of terror so abrupt and devastating they seemed to split time into 'before' and 'after'. I've seen famine carve hollows into the landscapes of entire nations and recessions crack the façades of the most confident economies. I've observed technological revolutions with the breathless awe of someone watching fire being discovered for the first time: the internet birthing a global mind, smartphones grafting themselves onto our palms, AI whispering strange new futures. A global pandemic proving that no matter how far we believe we've come, nature will always be the elder at the table. And through it all: the rises and the falls, the crescendos of human triumph and the deafening silence of its failures, I have *observed* – a witness to the remarkable, terrible, beautiful theatre of human history.

In times like these, it's easy to feel small and powerless. But *metta* reminds us that we are not without agency. We can still choose to send kindness into the world, not as some grand heroic act but as a deliberate offering, a signal, a refusal to go numb and lose our sense of agency. There's power in that, and we'd be wise to take it seriously. Because in this act of extending love, we draw closer to that part of ourselves that has never been wounded.

---

11. The Midday Moon

Act III begins much as Act II ended, with a chapter that contains the wisdom and reflections of my friend and mentor, Michael Harding. The essence of this chapter is distilled into a single sentiment from his words: 'Be still, and you will find that the very presence of the other person in the room no longer distracts you from meditation, but actually becomes the focus.'

In Act II, we turned our gaze outwards, letting the lakes, mountains and skies reflect the shifting tides within us – the thoughts, feelings and transient nature of our inner world. Now, in Act III, the focus tightens. The lens shifts from landscape to flesh and blood. You're asked to call to mind the one who holds the full weight of your love, not as a concept, but as a presence. Breath. Pulse. The gravity of them in the room. This isn't a distraction from the practice. It is the practice. They become the axis around which your awareness turns. Real, flawed, extraordinary. This was never meant to be solitary. It's always been about what exists between us. All the bonds, the tangle, the meaning we make in the middle of it all.

It's about making space – for them, for yourself – and letting love do what it does best: steady you and, when you're listening, answer back.

This chapter is personal. It was not something I wanted to share, but something I needed to write about. When you spend your time helping others navigate their way through, it's easy to forget where you are on the map. Writing this book was a pause. A moment to turn the lens inwards and ask, quietly, *What about me?*

THE PLACE THAT HAS NEVER BEEN WOUNDED

The title of the chapter comes from my childhood fascination with the moon lingering in a perfectly blue midday sky. On long drives as a kid, I'd badger my parents and siblings with the same question: 'Why hasn't the moon gone to bed yet?' They never had an answer, but I later learned that the moon appears during the day because it is always there, orbiting quietly, reflecting the same sunlight that brightens our world. Its presence during the day is no mistake but a reminder that light and shadow, day and night, coexist and shape each other. The moon challenges how we view opposites like joy and sorrow, teaching that they are intertwined. It is steady and unassuming, influencing the tides, softening the night, and grounding us, even when unnoticed.

It also reminds us of the people we love: those who orbit our lives, their importance often realised only when we pause to see them clearly or when they are gone.

This chapter is about noticing and appreciating the steady forces within and around us that shape who we are.

12. *Facts of Life*

Inspired by the words and spirit of one of Ireland's finest poets, Pádraig Ó Tuama, and his evocative poem 'Facts of Life', this section is an intimate reflection on what truly matters. In his poem, Ó Tuama dismantles the idea that life is built on grand gestures or glittering milestones. Instead, he invites us to notice the unassuming moments that drift by – the ones that, without fanfare, leave fingerprints on the architecture of who we are.

The poem avoids declaration but subtly redirects our focus to the transient details we often overlook and those small moments that, though seemingly insignificant, carry deep meaning. It stitches the mundane into something sacred, revealing the patterns that make the ordinary, extraordinary. It's about the connections we take for granted, the imperfections we try to hide, and the fleeting fragments of existence we rarely pause to acknowledge. These moments make life tangible, honest and layered with meaning.

Ó Tuama doesn't dress life up or smooth its edges but honours it as it is: flawed and achingly real. His work is a recognition that magic lives both in the remarkable and in the imperfect reality of being human.

It echoes the Buddha's teachings on impermanence, the central thread in both his philosophy and mindfulness practice. He taught that all things – material, emotional and mental – are always changing.

'You must accept change before you die. But you will die anyway. So you might as well live. And you might as well love. You might as well love.'

This chapter reflects on life's fragility and the constancy of love, the force that helps us face whatever change brings. With time and experience, I came to understand that impermanence is not an enemy. It is a teacher. And its most vital lesson is this: live life right here, right now, in *this* moment.

13. *Loving-kindness*

The foundations of *metta* meditation lie in one of the simplest yet most radical acts we can undertake – wishing well to others. First, those we love, then those around us, and finally, ourselves. In a culture that has accelerated towards near-nuclear levels of individualism, it's vital to remember that humans thrive in connection. We are at our best not in isolation, but in community. Recognising this and consciously offering our energy, care and presence to others is not just important, it's essential.

At its core, *metta* cultivates warmth, compassion and a sense of goodwill. It is not a mere intellectual exercise, nor a way to bypass the complexity of human relationships. Instead, it invites us to sit with the full breadth of our emotional landscape. Our joys and our wounds. And to offer care not despite these truths, but because of them.

For many of us, extending kindness outwards is far easier than turning it inwards. But *metta* teaches that to connect with the world truly, we must also nurture a relationship of compassion and acceptance towards our imperfections and humanity. From there, the circle widens to friends, acquaintances, strangers, and even those we struggle to forgive, and then finally to the entire universe, which so desperately needs that energy. It is a meditation on connection, a recognition that beneath all our differences and distance, we share the same hopes, fears and fragile longing to be happy and free from suffering.

The beauty of *metta* lies in its simplicity. It asks for no grand gestures or ornate rituals, only the willingness to sit, to breathe and to quietly repeat, 'I wish you peace,' 'I wish you health,' 'I wish you happiness.' It isn't about instantly transforming the world or denying struggle. It's a revolution of the heart. A practice of planting small seeds of compassion for others, yes, but also for yourself, that over time root into a stronger sense of connection. A shared humanity that holds all of us.

Metta was, without question, the practice that challenged me most. During our teacher retreats in Tullow I spent hours probing Helen, Jo and Paul, our master teachers, about the aspects that jarred with me. Forgiving those who had caused harm felt like a barrier I couldn't cross. I would sit with the memory of a teacher from my youth, his hand raised with that leather strap, and the fear he brought into my world. Visualising him seated before me and wishing him loving-kindness felt almost unbearable. But I stayed with it. I brought the Polaris principles into my awareness, and they helped me find the strength to hold space for that discomfort. Slowly, something changed – not a justification of his actions, but a release of their weight. I began to understand that forgiveness wasn't for him. It was for me. It wasn't about letting him off the hook. It was about unhooking myself.

Still, the part of *metta* that truly tested me was turning that same loving-kindness inwards. A dull, persistent ache arises when we confront the truth that, sometimes, it's far easier to offer compassion to a stranger than to ourselves. I've seen that ache in many of the people I've taught. The barriers we place between ourselves and our tenderness can feel immovable. That's why the Polaris principle of grace is so essential here. Grace invites us to open our space of truth and to receive the love we so freely give to others. It will challenge you, as it challenged me. But that's where its power lies.

As we enter the final practice of Act III, before moving into Act IV, I encourage you to let the music and meditation nurture you. The soundtrack was designed to hold you through the emotional terrain this practice may stir and to cradle you in the storm of vulnerability and healing.

This is a turning point in the journey. It asks much. But it offers so much more in return.

Chapter 11

The Midday Moon

But underneath everything is love.

So love is actually creating the space in which the other one breathes.

But when you have your eyes looking at the beloved, the other one in the room, and you are still, your consciousness is absorbing the other person.

So you're listening to them, you're paying attention to them, you're nurturing them so that the next second in their life will be the most beautiful.

Can I make the next moment for you be a moment of beauty?

I'm creating an awareness within which they are present.

I'm paying attention to them when they speak.

I am the universe around them.

I am their mother wishing that I could make the next second in their life the most beautiful experience they ever had.

How can I do that?

Answer: just be still.

Be still, and you will find that the very presence of the other person in the room no longer distracts you from meditation but actually becomes the focus.

Michael Harding

My younger sister Andrea's name lit up on my phone. A rare nocturnal appearance that made me pause. She's not one for late calls, which is exactly why it felt less like a chat incoming and more like a plot twist.

I'd just been dragged around the block by my Cane Corso, Stevie – 60 kilos of fur and blind enthusiasm. Calling it a 'walk' felt optimistic. I had one hand on the leash and the other carrying the industrial-sized poo bags being tested by Stevie's litter legacies.

There'd been a low hum of unease trailing me all day, a shadow I couldn't shake, and now my sister's call had come to cast it in full Technicolor. Her voice came through calmly but too carefully. 'Now, Niall, there's nothing to worry about . . .'

It was the conversational equivalent of tossing a grenade into a library. And for someone such as myself – an Olympic-level catastrophiser with a nervous system held together by string – it might as well have been the starting gun for a full-blown anxiety decathlon. She hadn't finished her sentence, and I was already drowning in existential dread sweat. In the background of her call, I could hear the unmistakable soundscape of a hospital: the faint beeping of machines, the shuffle of footsteps, disembodied voices. She pressed on, but her words came like sharp, clipped notes.

'. . . a bit of a complication with Mum's procedure. We're just waiting for the surgeon to come out and talk to us.'

A *complication*. A word that shouldn't even exist in the context of what was supposed to be a straightforward, routine procedure.

'It was only a fucking routine operation,' I muttered, primarily to myself, trying to wrestle my spiralling thoughts back into some semblance of order, like riot police trying to subdue a shower of chaos merchants.

Mum had gone in earlier for a heart biopsy. She'd been overtly nervous, which wasn't like her, so naturally, I did what every self-respecting doom enthusiast does: I googled it. In its cold, clinical wisdom, Dr Internet had assured me it was nothing. '*A minor procedure,*' it said. '*In and out in a few hours,*' it promised.

'There's nothing you can do here, Niall. We have to wait,' Andrea continued, her voice calm but firm, the way someone speaks when trying to steady a ship already taking on water.

I barely let her finish.

With Louize in the car, I was already on the M50, headed northwest towards the Hermitage Clinic in Lucan, about an hour's drive. The family WhatsApp was chaotic. Messages poured in relentlessly, and the constant buzz of my phone was a reminder of the unease ricocheting through our group. Every question, every half-formed thought, was funnelled straight to Andrea, the only one on the ground, absorbing the full weight of everyone's fears and unanswerable inquisitions. I couldn't leave her to carry it all on her own. I had no idea what I could do once I got there, but sitting still wasn't an option – moving felt like the only thing that made any sense. Even if all I could offer was my presence, just one more person in the room, I needed to be there.

I drove the journey in thirty minutes. Pulling into the hospital car park, I noticed my hands were shaking as I tried to take a ticket for the parking. It rattled me, considering I'm usually the person others look to when the figurative faeces meets the proverbial fan. My friends like to remind me, 'You're some lad for a crisis.' Maybe that's true. A part of me instinctively steps into that role as though it's written into my wiring. A saviour complex, maybe. Probably born from years of feeling like I couldn't save myself, so I turned the focus outwards. But now, I knew I had to check that impulse and rein it in. The last thing anyone needed was me storming in like an overzealous extra from *Grey's Anatomy*, demanding answers from surgeons. I needed to keep my head steady.

I found Andrea slouched in the reception area, her face a study of forced composure and sibling compassion.

'Any news?' I asked, even though I already knew the answer.

She shook her head slightly, confirming what little we'd pieced together so far: there was fluid surrounding Mum's heart. The biopsy instrument, the bioptome, had nicked her heart, throwing it into shock. Mum was in agony, barely able to breathe.

Mum hadn't wanted this procedure in the first place, and now here we were, living out the worst version of her fears. Sitting there, waiting to be allowed in to see her, I wrestled with my anger, trying to keep it from spilling out onto anyone who didn't deserve it. Behind the double doors, I caught snippets of hurried conversation before the surgeon finally emerged. He looked bruised and battered by his experience. His face was a ruin of exhaustion and shock; every line was carved deep, testament to a day that had unravelled into something unexpected and unholy. Oddly, I felt a flicker of empathy for him.

'This is such a rare occurrence,' he began, almost apologetically.

He explained that this had never happened to him before, a detail that, while truthful, didn't land with the comfort he might've hoped for. He continued that they were watching the fluid closely. Hopefully, it would drain naturally, but they'd need to operate if it didn't. 'We'll need to move your mother to the ICU,' he said, flatly.

'Will she be okay?' I asked, my voice heavy with hope and desperation, a question I was both terrified and compelled to ask.

And then came the moment that nearly undid me. He paused for a second and then did something I'll never forget. Without a word, he crossed his fingers on both hands and cast his eyes upwards, as if to appeal directly to some power beyond his control.

I felt the air drain from my lungs, the weight of that gesture hitting harder than anything he could have said.

'Can I see her?' I asked.

Hesitant, he nodded and went to speak with the nurse.

The nurse came out a few minutes later, and her expression was measured. 'She's not in a great state,' she said, gently. 'You might find it a bit of a shock.'

I didn't care. I had to see Mum.

The nurse guided me through the ward, weaving between an orchestra of beeping machines and monitors that made the room feel more like the insides of a Microsoft factory.

'She's stable for now,' the nurse added, her tone trying to land somewhere reassuring.

Mum is tough as nails and, even lying there, she tried to laugh as if to say, *I told you lot they shouldn't have come near me with that bloody biopsy.* But the scene was incredibly upsetting. She was half-naked, smeared with dried blood and vomit, her body slumped into the hospital bed. The nurse held a tray to her mouth as she retched, the morphine wreaking havoc on her stomach. Her blood pressure was dangerously low. I sat beside her, my hand resting on her bare back as she groaned in pain, her body trembling with every heave. I rubbed gently, doing everything I could to hold myself together.

The role reversal wasn't lost on me. This was the woman who had pulled me through my most vulnerable moments. Now, here I was, doing the same for her. As time seemed to pause, every other stressor in my life, every ounce of overwhelm, evaporated. Nothing else mattered. It was just the two of us in that room, the rest of the world muted.

I didn't patronise her with empty assurances like, 'It'll be okay' – I wasn't a consultant cardiologist last time I checked. All I could say, over and over, was, 'We're here with you.' And then, as if summoned by forces beyond my control, the words spilt from my mouth like verbal diarrhoea, startling even myself:

'Is this bed from IKEA?'

The nurse stopped mid-step, clearly caught off guard. 'I doubt it,' she said, raising an eyebrow. 'These beds cost tens of thousands of euros.'

Some mischievous soul had slapped an IKEA logo on the bed frame. 'Well, there's an IKEA sticker on the bottom of it,' I replied, with the charlatan-level confidence of Michael Scott.

And for the first time since I'd walked in, Mum lifted her head from the vomit tray. She didn't need to say anything – the look she shot me, which I had seen countless times in the past, translated perfectly: *Would you, for the love of all that is sacred, cease your incessant shite-talk, you insufferable fool?*

Still, it brought the faintest flicker of life back to her face. As the nurse later noted, it even nudged her blood pressure up a bit, which was positive.

They were moving Mum to the ICU, and the medics also needed to take her for a CT scan of her heart to get a clearer sense of the fluid build-up. It gave me a brief moment to step back, gather myself, and call the family, updating them on where things stood. As I sat in the ICU waiting room, watching six non-Irish medical staff caring for Mum, I felt a wave of gratitude consume me. A few weeks earlier, Dublin had been gripped by anarchic far-right riots, chaos spilling into streets I'd always seen as belonging to a kinder, braver city. It had left a bitter taste, a sense of a country I barely recognised. These caring medics, kind, steady and resolute, were precisely what Ireland needed, what we all needed. In the depths of my being, I hoped they knew how welcome, how loved, and how deeply appreciated they were. My family, and countless other families who had loved ones in need of their care, were indebted to them. The thought of leaving Mum sat heavy in my gut, knowing we couldn't stay. So I turned to the nurse, a kind face amid the whirlwind of machines and movement, and asked quietly, 'Please, take good care of her.' And they did. They truly did.

THE MIDDAY MOON

As we were leaving the ICU, the surgeon pulled me aside. His face was calmer now but still edged with the kind of gravity only a lifetime of life-and-death conversations could induce. He told me the CAT scan had showed the fluid was draining slowly but steadily. I felt relief loosen dread's grip on my chest, and he looked lighter, too. Yet his next words were careful: 'We'll need to monitor her closely over the next few days. Her heart has endured serious trauma.'

I nodded, more in reverence than reply, absorbing the full extent of his words. And yet, amidst the weight, I found air: the tremble in my hands softened and, for the first time in hours, I could breathe without feeling like I was borrowing it.

On the drive home, silence rode with me. Sleep felt laughably distant. The road unwound ahead, an ink ribbon of headlights and shadow, and though my mouth could've formed words, none seemed worth disturbing the charged silence.

Louize reached over and rubbed the back of my head as I drove. Her presence filled the unsteadying stillness with something more solid, something I could lean into. If nothing else, this night had shown me the ridiculous ways we squander our time, pouring energy into distractions and nonsense that, in the grand scheme of things, mean nothing. When it's all stripped away, what's left are the moments we spend with the people who give our lives meaning.

That night, I truly understood what a colossal waste it is not to be fully present with them.

We have carved a modern world from the stone of ambition, which swindles us into believing that contentment and happiness reside in the trophies of achievement and the weight of possessions. Yet the cruel irony is this: so much of what we strive for is done in the hope of making those we love – our parents, our guardians – proud.

THE PLACE THAT HAS NEVER BEEN WOUNDED

Recently, I spoke at a charity event in the States, and as I moved from table to table, introductions were made not with names or personalities but with report cards. 'This is my son – a straight-A student,' or, 'My daughter, top of her class,' they said, as if I should see their children through the prism of their achievements, like products on display at a sales conference. It struck me deeply that these children weren't presented as the objects of their parents' unconditional love, but as proof of their worthiness.

This is the landscape we've sculpted, a world where love is shadowed by metrics, where comparison has become our religion, where the people we cherish most are often invisible to us, unnoticed in their raw and beautiful humanity until it is too late; until something robs us of the choice to see them clearly and be present.

And then we're left to reckon with the hollowness of everything we thought mattered and the love we forgot to give.

Sometimes, offering love feels like trying to cup water in trembling hands – challenging, slippery and occasionally overwhelming. The people we hold closest, those we would move mountains for, can also be the ones who ignite us the quickest. Those connections have an emotional voltage, a charge that comes with love's depth and history. Life moves in cycles, and the dynamics of those relationships shift as we find our footing in the world. I remember, as a teenager, vividly wishing I could ship my parents off to some remote outpost in the northern wilderness of Canada. But now, in my forties, I would move heaven and Earth to sit in the kitchen with them, sharing tea and devouring whatever batch of buns my mother insists are 'healthy'.

'There's no sugar in these, Niall,' she'll say.

'Are you sure, Mum?'

'Well . . . just brown sugar.'

She's from the generation that believes any brown food must be good for you.

But those moments – the tea, the laughter, the warmth of their presence – are my sanctuary. They are my meditation. In those hours, no phones, emails or tasks claw at my attention. My mother and father are my breath. Life has a way of reminding us how fragile these moments are and how suddenly they can disappear. The thought of those cups of tea becoming a memory is enough to strip away the delusion that happiness is in academic results, accolades or success. Happiness is here, in the unbreakable connection of sitting across from someone who loves you without condition.

Of course, I know this isn't everyone's story. For some, the relationships with parents or loved ones are complex, fractured or even painful. But this isn't just about parents. It's about anyone who gives you that rare, unshakable sense of security and love. Those who make you feel held in the unpredictable chaos of life. Real presence and awareness are about opening yourself to the energy and connection of those around you, to the people who matter. There is nothing more profound, nothing more sacred, than being genuinely lost in the presence of another person, to feel them entirely, as if the rest of the world has melted away. In the vulnerability and fragility of life, do not take these people for granted. Cling to them, anchor yourself to their presence, because they are the truth of this existence. In the end, when the noise fades and the dust settles, it's them – it's always them. The rest is decoration. They are what matters. Everything else is just weather.

Mum left the ICU a few days later, her body mending but her spirit still carrying the weight of what had just happened. They had kept her in the hospital a little longer, and when I went to collect her, she was as I expected: a beacon in the ward, holding court with the other patients. Mum introduced me to her new best friend from the bed beside her like they'd known each other a lifetime.

As we walked out, she told me her friend's liver was failing and that she only had a few weeks left. I couldn't help but wonder who would sit at that woman's kitchen table when she was gone. Who would carry the rhythm of her presence? I hoped fiercely that her loved ones were drinking her in while they still could.

Mum was chatty on the drive home, relieved to be out of the hospital but carrying an understandable trauma, unspoken but palpable. The biopsy results hung over her like a shadow she didn't dare look at, not yet.

And then there was Andrena – Mum's sister, my beloved, beautiful aunt. Her fight with cancer was drawing to its inevitable, brutal close, over in Glasgow. The logistics of getting Mum over to see her seemed insurmountable. Mum had already lost her brother, Johnny, to Covid just a few years before. Now Andrena. Another sibling was slipping away. We didn't tell Mum any of this while she was in hospital; she needed her strength to focus on her recovery. But as the days passed, its weight sat heavier on us. I thought about Mum and Andrena, their cups of tea, their chats, their steadfast sisterhood. They'd been each other's sanctuary. And I thought about how Mum may never have another tea or bun with her sister . . . yet it didn't matter. When they were together, they lived *in the revelry of* each other, wholly absorbed in the moment, as if the rest of the world was the support act.

The week leading up to Andrena's death taught us all something about time, love, and how little we own of the people we hold most dear; they are lent to us by the universe. It was a lesson carved into the reposeful spaces between cups of tea, how they looked at each other, and how they laughed even as the world crumbled around them. It was a reminder that love is never measured in time, only in presence. Auntie Andrena was a presence — wry, warm, and unmistakably herself. I loved her deeply, and her absence has a peculiar weight. She never once missed a birthday card, as though time bent politely around her sense of occasion. She was, in every sense, the queen of Glasgow. Though given her well-documented disdain for the monarchy, she'd likely roll her eyes at the comparison and tell me not to be so bloody daft.

The pain, loss and trauma my mother experienced during that time was profound. There was no fixing it, no tidy resolution, only the simple act of standing beside her, holding her hand and being present in the pain. It felt like the only thing I could offer, and perhaps, in moments like those, it's the only thing that truly matters.

Weeks later, the biopsy results arrived: amyloidosis. This rare and often overlooked condition occurs when misfolded proteins (proteins that have become attached to organs) accumulate in the body and begin to interfere with its most vital organs: the heart, kidneys, nerves and liver. And in Mum's case, it was the hereditary form. We were all tested. Mercifully, none of us carries the gene for it — a welcome relief, tempered by the shadow it cast.

These experiences have a way of rearranging your sense of what matters. Of reminding you, sometimes more sharply than you'd like, to stay in the slipstream of the people you love. To move with them, not around them. To witness their pain, not solve it. And to know that, occasionally, love is less about what you say and more about being the grounding stillness someone else can lean against.

> **Audio track**
>
> When composing this piece, I was mindful of the weight of Michael Harding's words and what they meant; not just to him, but to me and perhaps to you. It felt essential to leave enough space for those words to land, to be heard, and to be truly embodied. I also had to tune in to how they made me feel.
>
> The first time I heard them, I was moved in a way I hadn't expected. For years, I had treated my practice as something deeply internal – an introspective space where I tuned out the world around me. But Michael's words shifted that perspective. They reminded me that presence isn't always about looking inwards. Sometimes, it's about looking outwards, about allowing those we love to become the object of our awareness.
>
> When my mother lay in that hospital bed, I couldn't experience anything but her. She wasn't just in my awareness, she was my awareness. Every breath, every glance, every moment felt magnified. And that's what this piece hopes to capture. I invite you to hold each word closely, to let them settle, and to allow them to become whatever you need them to be. That's your right – translating them into meaning that matters to you.
>
> The piano was designed to hold and heighten the emotional weight of those words – to elevate them and let them sink in. The take you hear in this recording was done in a single performance. It felt like my mother sat beside me, as she did when I was a child playing our Bechstein piano at home.
>
> The shift in melody at the end might feel dark, perhaps even melancholic, and in some ways, it is. But there's a release

that follows. A deep breath. A quiet realisation that, sometimes, the person sitting in front of you, the one you love, must become the very centre of your awareness. And in that stillness, there is both loss and healing: the reminder to embrace the presence of those you love, while you still can.

Chapter 12

Facts of Life

There was a trend doing the rounds online (so, not strictly peer-reviewed science) that claimed if you took the name of your first pet and paired it with your mother's maiden name, you'd arrive at your adult film star alias. By that logic, should the cinematic tides have turned differently, I'd be known as 'Bambi McElhinney'. And truth be told, it's not a bad name. Elegant, vaguely mysterious, yet professional.

Alas, that particular career path feels increasingly improbable these days. I've come to embrace the Lycra-loving, early-night-admiring splendour of my mid-40s. And let me tell you, if you've not reached this glorious age yet, don't rush, but do look forward. It's a blast. Less chaos, more clarity. And a bedtime you can be genuinely excited about.

I mention all this not because I intend to launch an OnlyFans account – perish the thought, the lighting alone would bankrupt me – but to introduce you to my first pet, Bambi. A Yorkshire Terrier, small enough to fit in a shoebox and yet somehow possessing a presence larger than most humans I've met, Bambi was the gentlest soul imaginable. Most nights, she would burrow under my duvet, curling herself into the warm crook at the arch of my feet, like a living hot water bottle with a heartbeat. We slept like that for years. Apart from my family, she was the first being I ever truly loved. I'd wake excited to see her each morning.

Though a nature-loving child, I have always had a deep affinity for animals. Like the land, they teach without speaking. Bambi was my first teacher in unconditional love. I could have burned the house down (and in my more hedonistic childhood chapters, it wasn't entirely out of the question), and she would still have sat beside me, licking my arm, as if to say, 'Ah well, we all f*&k up.'

The morning we found her lifeless on the porch, poisoned by a local farmer, was the first time I truly experienced grief. It was the first time my heart properly cracked. I didn't quite know how to express it at the time. But I remember this: it was the first time I felt the need to *protect* those around me. My sisters and parents were visibly shaken and unravelled in that helpless way only real heartbreak can cause. And so, instinctively, I made a decision. I wouldn't add to it. I swallowed my pain, not because it was small, but because theirs felt louder. I took on the role of the steady one, the calm one. It was my first lesson in emotional containment: that strange sense of duty to shield the people you care about from the weight of your sadness. And I carried that responsibility for many years.

But perhaps the most significant impact of that first collision with grief was the insidious narrative that began to take shape in my mind. *If this is how painful love can be . . . maybe it's best avoided altogether.* I wouldn't have had the words for it then, of course. But something in me decided that getting too close to anyone might be a risk that was not worth taking. If love could gut you like this, maybe distance would be safer. Cleaner. Easier to manage.

It's strange how childhood moments, mere fragments, can cast such long shadows into adulthood. You think you're just a kid losing a pet. But what you're doing is beginning to write the rules by which you'll later learn to love . . . or not.

But then someone sees you fully, as you are. They make space for the culmination of all your life experiences before they met you. That person for me, was Louize.

'I'm so sorry, I can't detect a heartbeat.' The gynaecologist's words hung in the air, heavy and almost untrue, as though spoken as a blatant lie by a shit-stirring friend. They felt distant, nearly mechanical, starkly contrasting the vivid reality unfolding before us. She pointed out our baby on the ultrasound screen – still and silent. Even as I write this, I feel myself spiralling back into that moment, trapped in its ravaging rawness. I can still vividly witness Louize's face, her eyes turning to mine as the weight of those words broke through our disconcerting, anxious haze. There's a peculiar agony in witnessing someone's heart shatter in real time, a cruel synchronicity as your own fractures alongside theirs. In that shared rupture, you feel the excruciating fragility of life and its haunting, fleeting beauty. Louize's grip tightened, her head falling into my hands. I kissed the top of her head, a pulsing, gentle, muted sob breaking the unearthly silence in the room. I felt her tears on my skin. It was an enigma I struggled to grasp. To feel so utterly broken and, at the very same time, transcendentally tethered to another soul.

The doctor, undoubtedly versed in giving such soul-crushing news, was professional and warm. She asked us if we would like a few moments. I attempted a response, my voice paralysed, before I saw her leaving the room. At moments such as these, I can become quite cerebral. I embrace logic and rationality over emotion. After the initial shock, a primal instinct to protect Louize replaced the acute despair. I don't know if I do this because of my habitual conditioning to run from pain or my innate sense of responsibility and compulsion to help others before even recognising what is unfolding within myself, much like I had done with my family when Bambi died. Louize broke the silence, a trembling cry of 'I am so sorry' shattering whatever pieces of my heart remained intact. I could not let her carry that, not for a second. The sole comfort I could offer at that moment was not just the declaration of my love but the weight of it, its presence.

Only half an hour before this, we had believed we would share this love with our baby. We'd spoken of the type of parents we wanted to become. We'd clung to the hope that parenthood wouldn't dissolve who we were, that we might welcome innocence without sacrificing the selves we'd spent a lifetime becoming. That morning, as we made our way to the hospital, the thought never even flickered that we'd return not with joy, but with a grief so sharp it would leave us fumbling to tell our loved ones that our beautiful baby hadn't made it.

When the doctor returned, her tone was steady and clinical as she guided us through the stark realities of what needed to happen next. She urged us to act quickly, her words efficient but not unkind.

Folks often speak of the emotional and psychological toll of losing a baby, but what seems seldom discussed are the physical consequences the mother endures. The body, like the heart, doesn't escape unscathed. As she explained the steps that would follow, I felt a tear I didn't realise existed escape and land on my arm. All I heard was that she had a slot tomorrow morning to proceed. Still, when she mentioned that another scan would confirm everything, a strange, naive hope moved in me – a desperate, fleeting belief that this could somehow be wrong. I had so many questions that it seemed like asking them might connect me to reality and make me feel less helpless and lost. Questions trick you into thinking you're solving something, into believing you're helpful in the face of the unbearable. I remember Louize fretting about a client she'd scheduled to meet the next day, worried about letting them down if she had to cancel. It struck me then, as it always did, how deeply her care for others ran, even when she was unravelling. That's the contradiction of her empathy – her boundless ability to feel, heal and understand others so profoundly that it almost eclipses her pain. It's what makes her the extraordinary psychologist and partner she is, though sometimes, heartbreakingly, it blinds her to her own delicate humanity and needs.

We floated from the room, shell-shocked and senseless about what had just happened. The receptionist asked us to fill out a form for the procedure. My hand shook uncontrollably, so she told me I could fill it out in the morning.

We needed to be back in the hospital the following morning at 8 a.m. to remove the foetus.

We had planned to grab some lunch after the appointment, but our appetites were stagnant, replaced by a wave of anxious, oppressive nausea. As we walked towards the car park together, Louize leaned on me with a heaviness that suggested she was struggling to stand upright. I pulled her closer, offering some emotional scaffolding. Couples nearby exchanged words that tapered into whispers as they noticed us, their faces showing a mix of sympathy and discomfort, hands instinctively moving to cradle stomachs as they hastened their pace, as if attempting to avoid being engulfed in that moment. I tried to muster a weak smile to express appreciation and perhaps vacuous reassurance that they would be okay.

Driving home, the dual carriageway felt endless. I gripped the wheel harder than I needed to, caught between anger and desolation. I would have to tell my family, and I dreaded the sound of their voices breaking under the weight of it. Thank God we hadn't announced it publicly yet, though that felt like the only mercy.

I couldn't bring myself to call my mum; the thought of her quiet pause, the way she'd take a steadying breath before speaking, was too much to bear. I knew how deeply she'd feel this, how her first instinct would be to shoulder it for all of us, and I couldn't bring myself to add to the weight she already carried. I texted instead. Quick, direct, as though brevity could shield her from the truth. I wasn't ready to speak because it would mean I had to accept it.

Louize, unable to find the words herself, sent a message to her family, a short note to say she'd call them later. I could only imagine the worry that would settle in the silence between her message and her call, how their minds would fill the gaps, so I reached out to her mother, sending a message to reassure her and let her know that Louize wasn't alone and that I would look after her. It felt small in the face of everything, but sometimes small acts are all we have to give. Often, they mean the most.

Just as we left the edges of Dublin behind, the thought hit me. My friend Shane Davitt, or Dav, as we call him, was already at the house. I'd asked him to help with a few things around the place, and being Dav, he hadn't hesitated. He'd driven three hours without complaint, with a toolbox in hand and that assured, capable way of his, ready to fix whatever needed fixing. He was like MacGyver – give him string, tape and a barrel of tea, and he could make miracles. But this? This wasn't something he could fix. I knew I needed to tell him before we arrived. Dav wasn't the kind of man you could keep in the dark; he would sense it when we walked through the door. And if anyone could be there in a moment like this, it was Dav. He is one of the best souls I've ever known; he has that rare gift of making heavy things feel lighter. As much as I hated him being caught in the middle of this, there was a strange comfort in knowing he was there.

That evening, we called our families. It wasn't the kind of conversation you rehearse for, but one that demanded a clarity and steadiness I wasn't sure I had. There were practicalities to address. Details about the surgery, the recovery period, and all the awkward logistics of navigating something you wish wasn't happening. Their questions came, thoughtful and precise, tinged with concern, but never panicked. And I answered them as best I could because they deserved that much. To know, prepare and share its weight in whatever way they could.

This situation wasn't uncharted territory for my family. That was the part that stung – not just the sadness of it, but the familiarity. And yet, within that sadness lay something unexpectedly grounding: a shared understanding. In a way, walking a dark path is more manageable when someone is walking it with you.

Neither of us slept a second that night. The doctor's words played on a loop while the image of Louize's agony spiralled through my mind. I did not let her go till our early morning wake-up, her hospital bag already packed and ready to go at the end of the bed.

There was an inescapable cruelness that defied words: people who had just lost their child had to walk through a hospital ward where newly excited parents stepped out, beaming, their arms full of balloons and flowers, their souls full of the promise of new life. A father pushed a pram, his pride almost tangible, carrying this precious bundle home to nurture and adore. An exhausted but glowing mother hugged the nurses, with doctors shepherding her through and wishing the new family well. And there we were, caught in the undertow of it all, clutching our grief as the world celebrated around us. One dad said, 'There goes my sleep for the next few years.' The words hung in the air, a casual lament wrapped in cautious joy, and I thought to myself, *I would trade sleep for the rest of my life if it meant carrying our baby out of this hospital.* It wasn't envy or anger that gripped me, just the crushing stark fact that the surgery ward where women came to have their lifeless babies removed sat adjacent to the ward where new parents cradled their newborns. Of course, it wasn't intentional. It was an old hospital, its layout more artefact than design. I said nothing to Louize; it was too raw, too glaringly obvious to bring attention to.

We arrived at the surgery ward, where they took us for a scan to confirm what we already knew. No heartbeat. Acceptance settled over us like a heavy fog, already too numb to let it hurt any more. The nurse's words were gentle but definitive. Louize's mum and sister, Lisa, had just arrived. I stepped away to meet them, trying to hold myself together, but I broke when I saw their faces. They were in bits, too. We stood there, sharing its weight, and I said we'd need to be strong when we went back up.

By then, they were preparing Louize for surgery. Watching her mum embrace her daughter in that moment was almost too much to bear. A love so fierce, so tender, colliding with the reality of loss. The four of us squeezed into the cramped hospital room, arms wrapped around each other, a small island of grief and resilience. It was heartbreak made tangible, but there was beauty in it, too, in the way we held on to one another as the world outside continued, indifferent.

The nurses arrived to take Louize for surgery. They told me it would be hours before she was out, so I could do nothing but wait. Yet another twist of unintentional cruelty: I had a keynote address to deliver that afternoon at University College Dublin – to a theatre full of doctors, no less. I let out a hollow laugh at its ironic absurdity. There was no backing out, no space to collapse under the weight of what had just unfolded. I don't know how I got through it. Every part of me wanted to stop, break down, stand before them and tell them everything. But autopilot kicked in, and I delivered the speech, each word a distant echo of myself. I finished it, but I'm unsure who they listened to, because it wasn't me.

FACTS OF LIFE

As I stepped off the stage, Louize's sister rang. 'Everything went okay, Niall. Louize is in post-surgery, recovering.' Her words were a lifeline. I mumbled my excuses, sidestepped the post-speech pleasantries, and locked myself in a cubicle in the bathroom. There I collapsed, as the last 24 hours – which had been some of the most painful of my life – crashed into me like a train.

People talk about primal responses to overwhelm: fight, flight or freeze. But there's another kind that takes you out of yourself. The world slows to a crawl, each second stretching impossibly thin. It's a floating detachment where nothing feels real, where you're lost in slow motion, suspended in a grief that refuses to relent. Driving back into the city, in a strange state of relief and sadness, podcasts were playing passively on the car speakers. The 'On Being' podcast with Krista Tippett was on, and she was interviewing the stunningly talented Irish poet and theologian Pádraig Ó Tuama. His voice and words captivated me. They were anchoring, inviting and affirming. He started to read one of his poems, 'The Facts of Life', as I parked the car outside the hospital.

That you were born
and you will die.

That you will sometimes love enough
and sometimes not.

That you will lie
if only to yourself.

That you will get tired.

That you will learn most from the situations
you did not choose.

THE PLACE THAT HAS NEVER BEEN WOUNDED

*That there will be some things that move you
more than you can say.*

*That you will live
that you must be loved.*

*That you will avoid questions most urgently in need of
your attention.*

*That you will begin as a fusion of a sperm and an egg
of two people who once were strangers
and may well still be.*

*That life isn't fair.
That life is sometimes good
and sometimes even better than good.*

That life is often not so good.

*That life is real
and if you can survive it, well,
survive it well
with love
and art
and meaning given
where meaning's scarce.*

*That you will learn to live with regret.
That you will learn to live with respect.*

*That the structures that constrict you
may not be permanently constricting.*

That you will probably be okay.

*That you must accept change
before you die
but you will die anyway.*

*So you might as well live
and you might as well love.
You might as well love.
You might as well love.*[7]

I closed my eyes as Pádraig's words settled over me. Sitting in my car outside the hospital, I felt unmoored, unsure of so much, but there were certainties I clung to, hooks of hope. My unyielding love for Louize, knowing she was safe, gratitude for her family and mine, and grounding in the smallest, most ordinary things. The poem's words weren't answers but were a harbour, a place to steady myself in the storm.

In Buddhism, there is a parable called the two arrows of suffering. The first arrow is the inevitable torment that visits us all, and no one gets out of it unscathed. The universality of suffering that applies to every soul that enters this world is part of our journey. The second arrow is the arrow that we fire at ourselves. The self-blame, the should-haves, could-haves, regrets, rumination, shame and wishes that we torture ourselves with. This arrow can rob us of the present moment and the certainties and stability that come with that awareness. We become buried in the ruins of time, stuck in a loop of yesterdays. We must resist the pull to unleash the second arrow, for the first has already found its mark and carved its scar. Why compound the wound with our own hand when the initial strike has already pierced deep enough?

There was a mirror in Pádraig's words and, in it, I saw the weight of my responsibility. Somewhere in the blur of the past,

I'd have seized on such moments as an excuse to indulge in self-pity, weaponising my hurt against the people who least deserved it. I could not, would not do that now. This self-awareness becomes a crucial ally on our path towards a place that has never been wounded. Self-awareness is the art of stepping outside yourself, like some detached, slightly amused observer, and watching the whole circus unfold. Your thoughts, your feelings, that knee-jerk reaction to the gobshite who cut you off in traffic, all of it. Not just the internal storm, but the way it leaks out into the world. This isn't navel-gazing; this is the bedrock of any real mindfulness practice worth its salt. When you create that space, that is the practice. Suddenly, you're not a puppet to your own wiring. You've got a choice.

Habitual responses and latent traits can creep back into our patterns of behaviours, especially during periods when that first arrow strikes us. They can bring emotional charges that remind us of a part of ourselves we would rather not recall. These moments can derail us. In such times, we must cling to our Polaris principles, our guiding truths, like a compass in the dark. Judgement and anger, sharp and blinding, have a way of obscuring the horizon. But with self-awareness, we can return to the journey that matters most.

The last few lines in 'Facts of Life' refrained like a hook in a great pop song: 'So you might as well live, and you might as well love.' The first arrow had already struck, harrowing and brutal, leaving its mark deep. I sat in the car, my hands trembling on that second arrow, but I wouldn't let it fly. What I could make sense of, with a clarity that cut through the fog, was my love and responsibility for the woman now lying in a hospital bed, drinking tea and eating toast after surgery.

And I wouldn't let her fire the second arrow, either.

That's the strange rhythm of life, mostly wonderful, stitched together by connection, but at times tragic and profoundly sad.

If we can learn to bear the pain of the first arrow, to let it pierce us without letting it consume us, we might find our way again. Let the scars form; let them heal. Let these words guide you as we walk this path towards the untouched, unscarred place within us. Allow yourself to get lost, stumble and feel the weight of confusion pressing down. There will be moments that feel impossibly sharp, pain that demands your full attention. Sit with it, not in judgement, but in self-awareness, grace, curiosity and patience. Take a break if you need to. But live anyway. Love anyway. Offer that love to yourself first, then to those around you who keep you standing when the world threatens to pull you under. There is a strange and beautiful truth in suffering: the thread binds all of us together. In a time when division seems louder than connection, bring yourself back to what unites us in the shared facts of life.

Across the years in my work and in my life, I have had the immense privilege of meeting souls who have endured levels of pain that most of us could scarcely comprehend. People who have stood, bloodied and battered, as arrows came at them from all directions, yet somehow, they kept moving forward. Their ability to endure and continue never ceases to leave me humbled. Witnessing such capacity to navigate adversity is, without question, the most incredible honour of my work: to see it, feel it, and be changed by it.

To those of you reading this, those who know all too well what it is to be struck by the arrows of suffering, I offer you my deepest respect and sincerest connection. Let us all learn the gentler art: to lay down the second arrow, the one we so often fire at ourselves, and in doing so, allow the first wound to heal. Your fingers will find the second arrow. That's the fight: not some future victory, but your hand opening, letting it drop again, and again. Until one day, you forget to reach for it at all.

Will you still fire that arrow sometimes? Yeah. Of course you will. This isn't about perfection – it's about catching yourself sooner. Dragging the weight of that quiver a little lighter each time.

So breathe. Aim lower. Miss deliberately. The target was never you.

Audio track

When I composed the music for 'Facts of Life' and paired it with the audio for this chapter, I focused on creating space – space for the words to breathe, for each syllable to land with weight and intention. The looping piano motif needed to carry a quiet hope yet remain deeply tied to the emotional gravity of the words. I wanted it to feel like your own voice, repeating these truths back to you; when Pádraig spoke his final words, 'You may as well love,' I was struck again by their simplicity and profundity.

I wanted the piano melody to reinforce the sentiment of those words. To represent that feeling of taking your hands off that second arrow, and allowing yourself to sit with the pain and suffering of the first one.

Chapter 13

Loving-kindness

*And when it comes – and it will come – never will
so many ask so much of so few.*[8]
Leo Varadkar, Taoiseach of Ireland

St Patrick's Day is not for the faint of heart. It's a marathon, a test of endurance that would make or break the most seasoned of revellers. For some, it's a green-soaked obstacle course where only the fittest (or most determined) livers survive – the milk-thistle month, as I like to call it. It's an unspoken tribute to the spirit of merriment as pints flow and cheers grow louder with each round. But to others, it's a day of profound significance, honouring a culture as enduring as it is proud. Beneath the boisterous clinking of glasses, parades and questionable costumes, a heritage has weathered centuries with grace and grit. St Patrick's Day is a day to celebrate a people who have faced history's storms with an unyielding spirit. A magnetising force that brings people together worldwide, no matter where they have ended up. St Patrick's Day, in its essence, is raising glasses, raising voices and carrying on Ireland's unbreakable heartbeat. And yet, with all our reverence, there's a little irony in how we celebrate. And as we pay homage to our patron saint, we conveniently leave out that St Patrick was Welsh. (Origin stories aside, he did his part, at least: chased the snakes out of Ireland; though if we're honest, a few might have slipped back in.)

But this St Patrick's Day was different.

COVID-19 had done the unthinkable: it had cancelled St Patrick's Day. That's when we knew this was serious business.

When Leo Varadkar, our Taoiseach (prime minister) took to the screen to address the nation, I was hunkered down in my parents' sitting room, fork in hand, picking at a macaroni and cheese that was more a block of cheddar than actual food. *If Covid doesn't get me*, I thought, *heart disease might very well finish the job.* The entire country watched Leo that night, faces glued to screens as if we were in some wartime broadcast.

The speech drifted, each word dropping like a lead weight into the room. Due to the 'severity of the numbers' and 'pressure on the health care system,' anyone over 70 or with underlying health issues was ordered to 'cocoon', a cosy euphemism for being sealed off from life. My parents, already feeling exposed, vulnerable and on edge, were now being told to become prisoners in their own homes. I could feel the air change, the slump of resignation, settling over us like stale dust.

I'd decided a few weeks earlier to come home and cocoon with my parents. I was the only family member who could work from home, so the job naturally fell to me. My ex-military dad had that indestructable, 'Sure, I'm invincible' streak, and if I wasn't there to keep an eye on him, I was pretty sure he would have been out licking counters and kissing strangers. And I was glad I came home. My uncle, Johnny, my mum's brother, passed from COVID-19 not long after that night, a short and brutal illness that left us in no doubt about the seriousness of what was coming.

I turned to my dad and broke the news gently that his daily stroll to O'Brien's for the paper was officially off. From here on, I'd make the ritualistic trek to fetch his paper and brown bread. He gave me a look, a strange cocktail of defiance and grudging acceptance, but didn't argue. When I returned with the goods, I'd scrub the paper down with Dettol, treating it like a radioactive relic. When I handed it over, headlines blurred, pages damp and frayed, it looked like a paper used to soak up an untrained puppy's piss in the kitchen. But he'd take it anyway, peeling apart the soggy sheets without a word.

I was terrified every day that I'd be the one to bring the virus through our front door. That fear seeped into everything: every doorknob I wiped, every surface I scrubbed, every breath I held around them, and every rogue sneeze. My parents and I joked that we used to cough to hide a fart, but now we farted to hide a cough. I tried to bury that anxiety in faux optimism, to keep things calm, but I think they felt it, too.

Ever the stoic, my mother embraced the grim reality of it all with resolve. I'd never felt closer to my parents than in those months, thrown together by strange circumstances in even stranger times. There was an unexpected intimacy in it, yet an undeniable loneliness. It was as though we were each trapped in our heads, grappling with what was happening, too shaken to reach out to one another. Conversations rarely ventured near the heart of things; instead, we drifted side by side, each trying to make sense of the chaos in solitude. When Mum's brother took his last, shuddering breath, my sister Julie, who'd been looking after him in Glasgow, sent a message to the family WhatsApp group. 'Johnny didn't make it,' it read. I was upstairs when I read it and found Mum hanging out the washing in the back garden as if the world hadn't just splintered. I went over to her and wrapped my arms around her, holding her as tightly as possible. She crumpled a little, her grief breaking through as she sobbed, though her hands kept reaching for the next piece of laundry. 'Good drying weather,' she managed to say. Dad, meanwhile, was up by the back hedge, trimming it as though we could bring Johnny back from death if he just managed to get a good shape on the bushes.

I felt a strange privilege being there for Mum when her brother slipped away. Even when we expect death, its arrival suffocates us, leaving a sadness threaded with guilt. His funeral was set for a week later, but we couldn't travel. Instead, we gathered around screens, watching the service on YouTube. On the day, I perched my phone on a rock by the edge of Lough Ennell, the waves lapping softly as I was eaten alive by the summer flies. The parish priest, alone in the church due to social distancing, gave a half-hearted eulogy while nodding off right in the middle of the Lord's Prayer. In fairness, he was used to being in a crowd. As I sat there, a local guard (policeman) strolled by and asked what I was doing outside the government's enforced 5 km radius. 'At my uncle's funeral,' I said, gesturing at the phone streaming it live. He gave me an empathetic look and said, 'This is nuts, isn't it?' And he wasn't wrong.

That time still feels surreal, a strange fever dream we were asked to push through without a moment to process. We were told to move on, to leave it unspoken, to bury the grief alongside the dead and keep going. And sometimes I wonder when, if ever, we'll allow ourselves to look back and make sense of it all. I worried about my family during that time. I could see the years slipping into their faces, lines deepening with every day of separation. My parents were heartbroken, longing to hold their grandson Billy and give him one of those world-famous hugs he was missing. Every visit became a painful ritual: Billy would sit in the backseat of the car, wailing from the driveway, begging to see his grand da and nana. 'I want to move to Australia!' he'd scream, his little voice breaking, having overheard that the *Crocodile Dundee* country was restriction-free. Too much for someone his age to understand, the innocence of it, mixed with his bewildered frustration, was almost too much to bear.

I worried that, without some focus or purpose, my parents would drift during this strange, suspended time. Dad had his golf and garden to keep him anchored, but Mum seemed occasionally lost, as if she was floating through each day; although Mum is like me, and quite comfortable in her own company, so I could see her embrace the solitude some days. She's always been an incredible musician, classically trained, a constant source of inspiration to me. I'd spent countless evenings as a kid sitting in the front room, listening to her play the violin or piano, her music filling the house. But arthritis had taken that joy from her hands, and she'd stopped playing. Seeing that part of her fade away was upsetting for me. I wanted to give her back a piece of that connection to music, something small but meaningful.

So, with a bit of hope and perhaps a dash of madness, I decided to buy her a ukulele, something her hands might handle, to lift her spirits over the months of lockdown. I hopped online, ordered her first ukulele, and pictured her rediscovering a bit of that old magic.

The very next day, a brand-spanking-new ukulele arrived via courier. Dad squinted at the box, commenting that it looked suspiciously small for a guitar. Bless him, Dad's a gem of a human, but our family's musical prowess didn't exactly trickle down from his side. His tastes are more, shall we say, unrefined. He's always been a Chas & Dave man, so I'm not entirely sure he was all that thrilled about the classical music operation Mum and I were cooking up on the ukulele front. Still, he humoured us, occasionally popping his head in to see what kind of racket we were making. As Mum plucked out her first tentative notes, I saw Dad's eyebrows lift in mild surprise.

Over the next few days, I could see the lightness the little ukulele was bringing back to Mum. She'd sit out in the garden, bathed in that rare, glorious sun, slowly teaching herself how to shape the chords and strum. Hours drifted by as she sat there, serenading the plants, her fingers dancing over the strings with determination. It was as though each note was bringing a piece of her back, something she thought she'd lost to time and painful joints. Of course, a few expletives escaped when she tackled the tricky F minor shape. But the whole garden seemed to listen and, I swear, even the flowers looked like they were leaning in to catch every tune.

I'd sit upstairs in my makeshift office, where I was working, feeling this immense relief as the sound of Mum's ukulele drifted up through the windows. She was finding something to carry her through the grief and the sheer boredom of it all. It eased something in me to know she had that small escape, a way to fill the strange emptiness that had settled over everything.

But her strumming got my chaotic mind whirring, too.

It made me wonder, if a simple ukulele could spark that glimmer in her again, what else might we find in all this madness? And suddenly, the days didn't feel so stagnant; they felt like they might teach us something.

I had an idea. And anyone who knows me knows these four little words are enough to make people run a mile. Frankly, I don't blame them. But there it was, a spark of something reckless and maybe slightly mad. I rang up my mate JP at the Musicmaker store, the guy who'd kindly sent the ukulele down for Mum. I asked him one very straightforward question: 'How many ukuleles do you have in stock, good sir?' (I've always believed that starting with an honorific sets the right tone for a conversation involving a significant request.) There was a brief silence on the other end. Eventually, JP returned with a cautious, 'Twenty, I think?' You could almost hear him wondering if he should put me on some watchlist. 'Right,' I replied. 'How much for all twenty?'

At this point, JP was genuinely questioning my mental state. And, honestly, so was I. But he did the mental maths, no doubt shaking his head, and gave me a quote of thirty euros a pop. 'Done,' I said, before I had a second to think about how exactly

I'd pay for this little venture. And just like that, I was in the ukulele business. Or, at the very least, in possession of a sizeable chunk of their Dublin stock, with absolutely no idea what I would do with it.

So I put up a social media post announcing that I had twenty ukuleles up for grabs, accessible to anyone stuck cocooning due to age or ill health. 'If you're feeling isolated and bored, these are yours,' I wrote. 'And I've even roped in a teacher to show you how to play the fecking things.' Justin, our guitarist from The Blizzards and one of the finest teachers I know, had stepped up without hesitation to do online lessons.

The response was ferocious. Within 90 seconds, every single ukulele had been claimed, primarily by families trying to bring light and purpose to their more vulnerable members. It was as if the whole community had been waiting for anything to break the monotony and remind them they weren't alone. And, suddenly, this little act of madness felt like it might be worth every cent I didn't have.

So I rang JP again. I wouldn't have blamed him if he'd thought twice about picking up. 'JP, how are you doing?' I asked sheepishly, dropping the 'sir' this time.

'Grand, until you called, you pain in the arse,' he shot back, understandably wary. 'Did you manage to get rid of those ukuleles?'

'I did,' I said, 'but here's the thing, JP – I need four hundred more.'

'How the fuck are you going to pay for them?' he cried.

'I have my ways, JP, sir.'

There was a heavy pause, and then the line went dead.

It was not exactly a shocker, as 400 ukuleles in the middle of a supply chain nightmare was like asking for unicorns. And even if, by some miracle, we did get them, how were we supposed to deliver them all?

But this idea stayed with me. If I've learned one thing, it's that persistence and a bit of madness might get us somewhere.

Remarkably, almost unbelievably, JP called me two days later. 'I've got those ukuleles,' he said.

Result. I'd never doubted his ukulele-hunting skills for a second.

That evening, I put another post up: 'Who wants a ukulele and fancies becoming a ukulele shredder?'

The only condition was that you had to be cocooning. I wanted these people to know they weren't invisible in this profoundly isolating time. We saw them, even if they felt cut off. In some small, strumming way, we were all still connected, and we were with them. I wanted to put the world's biggest ukulele band together during a global pandemic, and we would be called 'The Lockdown Ukulele Rockdown'.

Before long, we had over 400 ukulele novices from all over the island of Ireland, from all walks of life, in our makeshift band. All we had to do now was teach these brave souls how to play the little four-string wonders. That, thankfully, was Justin's department. But I felt we needed something more than just strumming practice – something to aim for, a proper goal. So, naturally, we decided to record a song remotely, with 400 people who could barely get through 'Wonderwall' on a ukulele ... bonkers, pure and simple. But, to be fair, I think Covid had driven all of us a bit insane by then.

The idea of hundreds of isolated, cocooning folks struggling through a tune together felt like beautiful chaos, and precisely what we needed to remember: we were all still out there, plucking away at something that felt like a connection. So, we picked a song, a cover version of 'Home' by Edward Sharpe and the Magnetic Zeroes. And we set off, teaching our rag-tag group to play their new instrument. Then came the challenge: they each had to record themselves on their phones and send me the video in four weeks. My job? Strip out the audio and stitch it into a coherent piece of music. I'll admit, it was brutal work. There I was, drowning in grainy, slightly offbeat ukulele clips, each one more endearing and off-key than the last. But as hard on the head as it was, there was something strangely moving about it, too. A beautiful messiness, each note a little flag saying, *I'm still here.* We even roped in Mum's over-seventies band, The Sweet Tunes, to sing the chorus, so now I had to mix all those voices in along with our special guests and the band. The whole thing turned into a chaotic production that nearly drove me to a nervous breakdown. But, somehow, there was a method in the madness. Each voice and pluck of a ukulele added its charm – a ragged, dissonant harmony from four hundred living rooms. It was sonic bedlam, but it was starting to feel real, strangely imperfect.

But, of course, now we needed a music video. You can't release a brilliant single without a great video to match. And how would we make a video during a global lockdown? No easy feat. We enlisted my mate Dec Murray, armed him with his trusty drone, and sent him flying into people's gardens across Mullingar. He captured them waving, dancing, strumming their ukuleles with each tiny performance pieced together like a mosaic of our collective musical anarchy: ukulele punks. Folks from all across Ireland sent videos of themselves in their gardens and sitting rooms playing their ukuleles.

And, somehow, against all odds, we pulled it off. The final cut was absurd and beautiful. It was a video stitched from backyards and balconies, and each screen lit up with faces smiling through isolation. It was messy and glorious, just like the times we were in.

But I should give a bit of context to this story, and, for everyone's sanity, explain that the moral here has nothing to do with ukuleles. Because, let's be honest, after this whole escapade, I'd be perfectly content never to see or hear another ukulele for as long as I live. The real heart of this mad project was something else entirely. It was about connecting people, giving them a lifeline in a time when all we could do was stay apart. Sure, it was clumsy, chaotic and involved a staggering amount of drone footage and off-key plucking, but it brought people together in a way I never could have predicted. So, if I've learned anything from this, it's that sometimes, in a world gone utterly insane, the only thing more ridiculous than a 400-person ukulele band is getting through Covid alone.

There is still so much we do not understand about mental health, so many unseen layers to the human condition that defy easy answers. But amid the complexity, there are things we do know. The consistent and compelling evidence tells us that strong, connected, respectful communities lie at the heart of positive mental health outcomes. We thrive not in isolation, but in belonging.

Another hare-brained attempt at salvaging the spirit of things took shape during that first pandemic Christmas: a Christmas, we were told, like no other. The Irish government had spoken, and the decree was explicit: tinsel and turkey, yes; togetherness, absolutely not. And so, as the world braced itself for a holiday stripped of its very essence, my thoughts turned to those for whom Christmas had always been less about the grand festivities and more about a single, irreplaceable thing: presence. To feel vulnerable is one thing. To feel vulnerable and alone at a time when the world is supposed to close in around you in a blanket of love is quite another. And so, I found myself wondering, what could be done?

I thought of the men and women in nursing homes, scattered across my town and indeed the whole of Ireland, who would find themselves staring at empty doorways where their children and grandchildren should have been. No warm embrace, no familiar chatter.

I sent out a few messages to my musician friends, and before long, what started as a passing thought turned into an actual plan. It was a mix of good intentions and last-minute scrambling. The idea was simple: take to the road, stop outside nursing homes and hospitals, and play music for those who had spent far too long staring at the same four walls. Stages? Improvised. Sound equipment? Sorted. And just like that, the World Tour of Mullingar commenced.

I wouldn't fault you for questioning the wisdom of it all. The last thing these poor souls needed, amid a global pandemic and the twilight years of their lives, was some bleary-eyed lad caterwauling a tune on a battered guitar with all the tuning precision of a rusted gate hinge. Fear not. There was, I assure you, an element of quality control. Marginal, but present.

We took our world tour across Mullingar: gardens, hospital car parks and nursing home driveways. It was chaotic and heartwarming. I was also recording a podcast episode along the way, which turned out to be a logistical mess. I wasn't allowed into any of the homes (understandably), so I interviewed the residents through the windows with my Zoom recorder, like some sentimental spy.

I asked everyone the same question: 'What matters in life?'

Everyone said the same thing: family, friends and the people you love.

Except for one lad, who just leaned in and said, 'Whiskey and women,' in his best Father Jack impression. Who was I to argue with that?

But irreverence aside, there's an experienced wisdom in their answers: one we'd do well to listen to. I could've asked them to choose between winning the lottery or spending more time with the people they loved, and they'd have picked the latter without blinking – apart from Father Jack.

As the weeks of the pandemic effects bled into months and then into years, it became painfully clear that we were in for a much longer haul. At some point, it dawned on me that we needed another project, partly for the community, but if I'm honest, just as much for my sanity. Fortunately, this time, fewer ukuleles were required. None at all. This one was *a cappella*. We decided to bring together all the schools in Mullingar, every choir that would listen, and anyone else willing to return our calls, to produce a version of 'Caravan of Love', performed by the Housemartins. Everyone was welcome. Videos were recorded, harmonies layered, and out into the world the song went. The response was extraordinary.

We live in a world that often celebrates rugged individualism and prizes self-preservation over shared experience. This cultural pull towards disconnection, towards 'doing it alone', contradicts everything we know about what makes us well. It is a contradiction at the centre of modern life. If we are to care for our collective mental health truly, we must gently but firmly resist the myth that we are meant to face life unaided. Community is not a luxury. It is a cornerstone.

The inspiration behind these three projects was rooted in one of the core foundational ideologies of mindfulness practice. *Metta* meditation, or loving-kindness meditation, has been one of the most impactful experiences in my learning and teaching. It's a simple practice on the surface, but it pulled me out of a narrow, ego-driven view of the world. It opened my eyes to the invisible threads that connect us, the social fabric that holds us together, often unnoticed.

During those strange, silent lockdown days, that connection felt clearer than ever. The illusion of separation cracked. Covid stripped away decades of polished individualism, leaving us exposed, but also, somehow, closer. I found myself feeling connected not just to family and friends but to strangers I'd never meet. It felt like the world remembered that 'it takes a village' for a brief moment.

Metta is a practice of opening the heart.

I wish you peace, I wish you health and I wish you happiness.

It sounds simple, maybe even soft, but it does something tangible. It shifts your perspective. You extend those wishes outwards to loved ones, acquaintances, and eventually to people you struggle with or have had conflict with before, then offer them to the world. Finally, you offer it to yourself.

It's not about pretending everything's okay. It's about recognising that underneath all the noise, most of us just want the same things: peace, safety and a little happiness. *Metta* gently wears down the barriers we build around ourselves. In the solace of meditation, you realise how much energy goes into holding them up. For a few moments, you feel that connection, not just intellectually, but physically. You remember that we're all navigating the same messy, beautiful chaos.

It's grounding. Not dramatic, not dazzling – just spiritual. It reminds you that you don't have to carry everything alone.

In a culture that sometimes thrives on division, where algorithms feed outrage and strangers feel like enemies, *metta* offers an alternative. It reminds us that most people, deep down, wish each other well. By building compassion inside ourselves, we change how we move through the world. It ripples out.

Ironically, the hardest person to direct kindness towards is often ourselves. We can wish strangers well but hesitate regarding our hearts. It feels awkward, maybe even undeserved – *I wish myself peace, I wish myself health and I wish myself happiness* – but *metta* asks us to keep going, to soften, to believe that we, too, are worth that kindness. With the support of the Polaris principles,

THE PLACE THAT HAS NEVER BEEN WOUNDED

we start to embody this energy of *metta*, and we become more able to lift others.

This isn't a solo journey. We need each other. Love, in the end, is energy. We can offer it, or withhold it. *Metta* is the decision to offer it, without conditions. And in that choice, something moves us. It becomes an act of resistance against a world that often tells us to guard ourselves instead. I saw this in real time. Watching 400 ukuleles travel across the country to people I'd never met, people I likely never will, was a lesson of compassion in motion. The joy on their faces, knowing someone saw them, cared for them, and reached out, was an emotive experience. That was *metta*. It was not abstract, not a spiritual theory, just kindness, shared between strangers in a time of deep isolation.

In that act, we reminded each other that kindness is still out there. It's everywhere. Each of us has the ability, and maybe even the responsibility, to share it. To let it move through us.

Knowing that others, friends, family, and strangers, genuinely wish you well? That's fuel. That's a strength. It carries you back to the part of yourself that's untouched by hardship. The place that endures. The place that has never been wounded.

Audio track

The *metta* meditation and accompanying compositions in this chapter resonate with me particularly. They represent more than just sound or practice: they are expressions of connection. I recorded the piano track in a single, continuous sitting – no edits, no retakes. I wanted it to feel lived-in, human and honest. The aim wasn't perfection; it was presence. I hoped to create a space large enough for listeners to step into fully, to carry the energy of loving-kindness – not to distract or entertain, but to hold a sonic sanctuary. To ground you. To guide you inwards.

While playing, I pictured people: loved ones, strangers, friends, standing across from one another. I imagined the words of the meditation passing between them not as abstract ideas, but as something observable. The refrain is simple by design, repeated with care, so that its message might be absorbed rather than just heard. To that end, I'd ask you to listen not just with your ears, but with attention and with that deeper part of you, the space of truth. These pieces are offered in the spirit of kindness, not as instruction but as invitation. Let the words and the music meet you where you are.

You may find that as you listen, something softens. That you feel less alone. That the harsh edges of the day become a little more manageable. If it does nothing more than help you pause, just for a moment, and connect with that place in yourself that remains untouched by the world's noise, then it has done what it came to do.

Metta is not a grand gesture. It's a return. A reminder that beneath all our differences and distance, something is still shared. And sometimes, all we need is a way to remember it.

I wish you peace, I wish you health and I wish you happiness.

Act IV

The Place That Has Never Been Wounded

There's an amazement that loops in my head like a scratched record: the staggering truth of what we are all capable of.

When I was young, I knelt at the altars of athletes and musicians. We called them 'geniuses' and 'legends' as if it were magic, not sweat, that made them gods and goddesses. As if they weren't made of the same blood and fractures as the rest of us. In those years, I was convinced these people existed on some higher plane – untouchable deities whose godlike talents could never be grasped by a mere mortal from Mullingar, marooned in the middle of Ireland. And I fear so many of us are ensnared in the same delusion: the fallacy of the anointed, the myth of the extraordinary life. We are bombarded daily with 2,796,463,731 Ways to Live Better! – each one peddled by well-intentioned gurus who mistake their own homogenised success for universal truth. Their sermons, amplified to nuclear scale, sear into our senses until we forget the divine power of simply *being*.

For me, now, after all the pitfalls and prizes, the highest achievement in life isn't virality or virtuosity. It's presence. It's connection. It's the unglamorous, unoptimised act of existing without apology, of resisting the tyranny of more. To stand still in a world spinning madly, is, perhaps, the rarest rebellion of all. The people who fascinate me now? The ones who build floors under feet, not pedestals; who stitch community from nothing but grit and care – you. The tragedy isn't that we don't see their worth; it's that they're usually the last to see it in themselves. You want to witness greatness? Look in the mirror. Then look past your shoulder at the ordinary miracles keeping you alive.

This book, in many ways, has been an exercise in sitting across from you at a dimly lit kitchen table, handing over the pages of my life – not just the triumphs (though I'll gladly take those), but the stumbles, the face-plants, the moments where I had to scrape myself off the floor. I wouldn't change a second of it. Not the dizzy highs, not the knuckle-whitening lows, because all of it led me here, to this conversation with you, to two people leaning in, saying, *You too? I thought it was just me.*

For twenty-five years in the riotous carnival of music and creativity, I've held on to one undeniable truth: an audience isn't a faceless mass. They're individuals. You're an individual, with your battles, your victories, your nights staring at the ceiling, wondering how the hell you'll get through tomorrow. And when I write or perform or speak, I'm not doing it to hear my own voice. I'm doing it because somewhere along the line, a song, a book, a few honest words from a stranger pulled me back from the edge. That's the contract. That's the magic. Art, at its best, is a hand reaching out in the dark, saying, *Grab on. We'll walk together for a while.*

Although we so often linger on the wrong side of the greener grass in our minds while measuring our worth against the gilded illusions of a celebrity culture, there remains something we alone can grasp, steer and navigate. It is the agency to live from a place of presence, that rooted ground beneath the noise. Now, let me be clear: this is no small feat. But the hardest things in life grow lighter when we reclaim even a sliver of control within their realm. By picking up this book, you've already made a choice: to either deepen your roots in that stillness or to seek the path back to it when the world shakes you loose. This is the pursuit of the unbroken place within you. The part that has

THE PLACE THAT HAS NEVER BEEN WOUNDED

never been wounded, never been less than enough. And if that sounds like folly in an age of endless distraction, well, then folly might be the wisest compass we have.

Which is why, as we near the end of this particular journey, as we begin to brush our fingers against that untainted, unbroken place within, I want you to know: this last stretch isn't about me any more. It's about you. Not in some vague, inspirational-poster way, but concretely, practically. What will you take from these pages? How will you carry it into your life, your relationships, your mornings when the alarm goes off and the world feels heavy? That's the agreement we're going to make here. Not that I have answers for you, but that I trust you to find your own.

And if there's one thing I hope lingers after you close this book, it's this: you matter. Not as an abstract idea, but as a living, breathing, gloriously imperfect human. Your story counts. Your voice matters. And wherever you go next, you take this with you, not because I said so, but because it's always been true.

As a mindfulness teacher and educator, you can sense it from those coming to the practice for the first time, or having reached the end of their patience – that cocktail of hope mixed with exhaustion. They've been running on life's treadmill so long, they've forgotten what solid ground feels like. And now here they are, hands slightly trembling with the vulnerability of asking:

How long should I practice?
When is the best time to meditate?
Am I breathing right?
Should I kneel or sit?

These aren't trivial questions. They're lifelines thrown by people who've spent years, maybe decades, being told they're doing life wrong. Of course they want instructions. Of course they crave a map. When everything else in life comes with a manual, why wouldn't so-called enlightenment? When I tell them, 'There are no rules,' I observe their faces. Some bristle – they came for answers, not riddles. Others exhale like they've been holding their breath for ever. Because what sounds like dismissal is an invitation: 'You cannot fail at this.'

I'll say that again.

You cannot fail at this.

Mindfulness isn't another performance to perfect. It's not about hitting some spiritual high score. Those questions about timing and technique? They're just the mind's last desperate attempt to turn presence into another achievement to chase. But the secret your anxious mind doesn't want you to know – that moment when you catch yourself thinking 'I'm doing this wrong?' – that's the practice. The sigh when the timer goes off after what felt like eternity? That's the practice. The fidgeting, the frustration, the glorious mess of it all – that's not failure. That's you showing up. That's the route. So yes, sit for however long feels honest. Breathe however your body wants to breathe. Come when you can. The door isn't hidden – it's been open the whole time. You were too busy looking for the key to notice it.

And so I offer you the same advice I've learned through trial and error, through stiff mornings and a back that's seen better days. I can tell you this: I find sitting in the morning light helps ground me, when I can manage it. More often than not, though, I'm flat on my back because decades of reckless abandon have left my spine with opinions of its own. Walking meditations? A gift, especially when the world outside feels more alive than the chatter inside my head, and time is tight on a busy day. What works for me may not work for you. This isn't about mimicry; it's about discovery. Mindfulness is a skill, and like any skill, it develops with practice – not perfection nor intensity, but with consistency. Some days, that means formal meditation. Others, it's losing yourself in a conversation so deeply you forget to check your phone, or standing before a piece of art that steals your breath and pins you, gently, to the present moment. The real value isn't in the *how*, it's in the *doing*. So find your balance. Your rhythm. Your own way home to the place that's never been wounded.

With this in mind, let us return to the Polaris principles from Act 1. Let's begin with 'non-judgement'. Cast your mind back to those fuck-ups and break-ups, the moments of madness and mayhem that litter all our pasts. How quickly, how reflexively, you reached for the gavel of judgement, sentencing yourself to a prison of 'should-haves' and 'if-onlys'. There's a fine line between taking responsibility for ourselves and punishing ourselves with misguided judgement. And how this tendency amplifies in the sacred, silent space of meditation! There, judgement slinks in like an old, unwelcome guest, making itself at home in the corners of your mind. There's a sort of comfort to it, sometimes, a grim familiarity, a knowing, because we've grown so accustomed to its weight we've memorised the script it recites: 'You're doing it wrong. You're not good enough. You'll never get this right.'

But the invitation here – the punk rebellion, if you like – is that as you stride and stumble towards that unbroken place within, whether in formal practice or the informal theatre of daily life, try this: *Hold the judgemental mind in awareness.* Observe it, not as a truth, but as a passing cloud; a thought, not a commandment. And then, see if you can carve out a sliver of space between its arrival and your response. Respond, don't react. That's the first step.

With consistency, something remarkable happens. Judgement, that tireless critic, grows jaded. It burns itself out, like a tantrum-throwing child who realises no one's listening any more. Its occurrences become rarer, its voice quieter. And in that is peace.

Modern culture thrives on noise. Withdraw anyway. Study the silence. Return to the fray only when the silence has taught you something. Then, and only then, will you move through the chaos with certainty. Not as a spectator, but as part of the collective. Where you, and every other soul, belong.

The Polaris principle of 'untethering' is an ally that's stood by me more times than I can count on this ragged, glorious journey. I've come to realise that one of my most reflexive (and, frankly, exhausting) strategies for countering the rampaging beast of anxiety was to chase control. Panic attacks feel like the utter annihilation of control. So, for years, I convinced myself that the antidote was to grip the reins of everything – professionally, personally, socially. Work, love, and even play became meticulously managed territories. And it made my world small, suffocating and devoid of colour. I envied those 'fuck-it' souls who flung themselves into the unknown with ease.

Maybe you've felt that envy, too. In a world that often feels like it's spinning off its axis before we even factor in our own messy lives, it makes perfect sense to crave a cocoon, a safe little bubble where we know exactly what's coming and can sidestep anything unpleasant. But the irony is that the very cocoon feeds the panic. It hands anxiety a megaphone and makes the impossible possible in your mind. In mindfulness meditation, we often try to apply the same flawed logic. We have an allergy to the uncomfortable, the intense, the prickly sensations, while clinging desperately to the serene, the pleasant. We become almost co-dependent on them. In the wild, uncharted terrain of your inner world, you never know what you're going to stumble across. A memory? A tidal wave of emotion? A bizarre, half-formed thought about what you'd name a pet capybara?

You've been there. You know this. So here's what I ask of you, gently, but firmly: 'Let go.' Unshackle yourself from that entirely understandable, deeply conditioned need to dictate the experience. Observe it all – the storm and the stillness, the chaos and the calm. Control is an illusion. And the moment you stop fighting to maintain it, you might find something far more powerful waiting for you.

The novice soul demands something far more challenging than nostalgia. It requires you to reactivate your capacity for ruthless attention. There was a time when your entire being could lock on to a ladybird climbing a blade of grass with the intensity and curiosity of a scientist making a breakthrough discovery. That wasn't childishness; it was your birthright of engagement with the world, before you traded it for the false efficiency of half-lived experience. Look at your life now. When did you last stop dead because something commanded your focus? Not for content, not for show, but because of the thing itself – the way light fractures through a dirty window, the precise mechanics of your own breathing. We've been trained to treat these moments as interruptions when they're the only moments we're truly alive. This is where the Buddhist idea of the beginner's mind becomes revolutionary. When the old familiar dread rises during meditation, you have a choice: the well-worn path of resistance ('This shouldn't be happening') or the unexplored territory of investigation and curiosity ('Show me exactly what this is'). Do it as active interrogation rather than passive acceptance – locate the exact coordinates of sensation, feeling. Replacing the 'I don't like this' with 'Isn't this interesting? I wonder why I am sensing this here?' softens the experience. The novice soul can strip away your stories about reality. Your anxiety stops being 'my weakness' and becomes a pure physiological phenomenon. Your distraction isn't 'failure' but an observable neural activity.

The difference is tectonic, the method simple. When you catch yourself sleepwalking through another day – body in one place, mind in fifteen others – stop. Stop intentionally, and invite curiosity. We never lose this ability – we abandon it. The novice soul is the part of you that still knows how to see what's there rather than what you expect to see. And in a world drowning in manufactured experience, your real experiences have never been more important.

This is where we need to reclaim our own authority – not by rejecting the available technology that is all around us, but by putting it in proper perspective. The real benefits happen when we use these tools as starting points for deeper inquiry. When a 'poor recovery' score becomes an opportunity to ask: *What does my body actually need today?* When a 'great sleep' rating still leaves you foggy, prompting you to consider: *What else might be affecting my energy?* Tomorrow morning, try this: before checking any device, take thirty seconds to scan your physical reality. Notice your breathing. Assess your energy. Feel into your muscles and joints. Then look at the data – not as gospel, but as one piece of a larger puzzle. Because no algorithm can account for the complexity of your life, no wearable can measure how meaningful work fuels you, or how stress lingers in your shoulders, or how joy gives you wings. These are things only you can know.

The most sophisticated technology we'll ever have is the one we were born with – this miraculous human system that's been communicating with us since our first breath. Our job isn't to outsource that wisdom, but to refine our ability to *listen*. The body scan meditation that is attached to the audio soundscape for this chapter helps us to tune back into the credence frequency to do just that.

THE PLACE THAT HAS NEVER BEEN WOUNDED

One of the great privileges of this work of sitting across from hundreds of souls, each wrestling with their own beautifully human contradictions, is spotting the universal threads woven through all our struggles. We may wear different faces, carry different stories, but so many of us share the same curious affliction: an almost reflexive inability to extend to ourselves the kindness we'd lavish on a stranger. There's a particular moment that arrives, sooner or later, in every honest person's journey – a jarring realisation that you've been treating yourself like an opponent rather than an ally. If you're reading this, I suspect you know it well. How many times have you taken rejection, failure or heartbreak and weaponised it against yourself? How often have you absorbed professional setbacks or personal stumbles as proof of some fundamental inadequacy? *I deserved this. I'm lacking. I'm broken.* What's fascinating isn't that we do this, but that we do it while knowing better. We'd never tell a grieving friend they're 'weak for still hurting'. We wouldn't dismiss a loved one's exhaustion with 'sort your shit out'. Yet when it comes to our own stumbles, we so often appoint ourselves judge, jury and executioner.

The goal isn't to eliminate struggle; it's to change your relationship to it. To meet your own mind not with a clenched fist, but with what a friend calls 'the dignity of a raised eyebrow' – that amused recognition of '*Ah. There I go again.*' And then, the conscious choice to continue anyway, not because you're flawless, but because you're trying. After all, what could be more human than that?

The Polaris principles are not instructions. They are coordinates. Their application, their timing, and their weight belong entirely to you. Acts 2 and 3 become, then, not a map but an excavation: what, in your hands, constitutes the mountain? The lake? Where do you locate beauty, or truth? Who stands in your orbit, fully present? This is agency. And when you wield these

THE PLACE THAT HAS NEVER BEEN WOUNDED

principles, you acknowledge the self you once knew without question, before life made you doubt its presence. It did not leave. It could not. It endured what you endured. You are remarkable, not as a platitude, but as a fact.

Every book arrives at this moment – when the writer must account for its existence. This one could not settle for theory alone. It needed to be useful – a tool, not just an idea; something you could hold in your hands, apply to your days, and return to, long after finishing it. But words, no matter how carefully chosen, have their limits – some truths are felt before they're understood. That's why I created the sonic soundscapes to accompany this book. The compositions are the unspoken half of every principle in this book. They are the emotional undercurrent, the resonance that lingers when explanations fall short. Music has always been my way of reaching what I couldn't name, and now it's yours. Every piece was written with deliberate care, from a place of deep respect for the work we're doing here. Nothing was composed lightly. Nothing was included without purpose. This music is an invitation to remember, to return, to trust that the unwounded self is not an abstraction, but a fact. Return to it when the world feels small, or when you need to remember what solid ground sounds like. Play it in order, or follow intuition's pull; some days will demand movement, others stillness. Let it be what you require: meditation, refuge. When everything outside grows deafening, these sounds will hold fast, not as escape, but as homecoming and rediscovery.

I wrote this book first for the unrefined catharsis of truth-telling. Not healing, not wisdom, but simply the bone-deep need to chart the coordinates of my own becoming. Some people flinch from such excavation. I have come to find it my only compass. And of course I wrote it too for you, reader. Not to offer false comfort, but to stand witness to the fundamental human paradox: we are each alone in our skin, yet bound together in our imperfection. If these pages do their work, you will feel less like a problem to be solved and more like a person who is already whole.

And finally, I wrote it for my father. So he would finally accept and realise that I *was* MEDITATING.

Notes

1 Erving Goffman, *The Presentation of Self in Everyday Life* (New York: Doubleday, 1956)
2 Jack Kornfield, *The Art of Forgiveness, Lovingkindness, and Peace* (London: Ebury, 2002)
3 Julianne Clarke, 'Restore 1304 crosses and grave identities at St Lomans [sic] Hospital Mullingar', Uplift, https://my.uplift.ie/petitions/restore-individual-grave-markings-at-st-lomans-hospital-mullingar
4 Alan Watts, 'Coincidence of Opposites', in *Tao of Philosophy* (North Clarendon, VT: Tuttle Publishing, 1995)
5 Rumi Network, *The Essential Rumi Quotes*, trans. Shahram Shiva (n.p.: Rumi Network, 2023)
6 Rob Reiner (dir.), *This Is Spinal Tap* (UK: Spinal Tap Productions, 1984)
7 Pádraig Ó Tuama, 'Facts of Life', in *Sorry for Your Troubles* (Norwich: Canterbury Press, 2013)
8 Leo Varadkar, 'National Address by the Taoiseach, St Patrick's Day', 17 March 2020

Acknowledgements

To those I love, your presence is all I need to navigate the chaos of this world. Though I may not always be as present as I'd like to be, you are never far from my mind.

To my beautiful, empathetic and emotionally intelligent family, friends, pets and community – you are all gifts. To my girls, Louize and Stevie, you help me find that place within me that has never been wounded, every single day. I love you all.

Writing a book is challenging. Writing an album to accompany it is even more so. You can't do this kind of work alone. I'm endlessly inspired by the talent and craft of those in the creative industries. I know I can be a little chaotic to work with, but I never take your patience for granted.

Harriet and Glenn at CAA, Jonathan, Dom and Eleanor at JMP – thank you. To my co-producer Eliot James, and longtime collaborators and friends Aidan Cunningham, Dara Quilty and Joe Egan, your creativity and friendship continue to lift me.

To those who creatively keep me honest, honour my vision, and have been such joys to be around – Andrea Cullen, Tanya Cullen, Isaac Burke and Conor English – I'm so grateful for your energy and belief.

And of course, to my creative force of a record label, Inni – and Colm, Willy, Jon, Matthew, Atli, Úna and Louise – thank you for believing in this project from day one and for carrying its spirit with such care.

To those who've offered wisdom and learning over the years in academia, life and work – the steady voices that guide us when the world feels shaky: Michael Harding, Tony Bates, Nóirín Ní Riain, Pádraig Ó Tuama and those who have come before – your words make a divided world feel less divided.

To those who have allowed me to wander through my creative world while keeping the show on the road in my other passion – teaching our kids to become better guardians of their own minds – thank you.

Paula, Colm and every single person who has dedicated their hearts to the same mission at A Lust for Life, I'm deeply grateful.

I could go on. But for now, let me thank you for your trust, your time and your presence. My hope is that somewhere along this journey, you rediscover that place within you that has never been wounded – and remember, it never truly left you.

Access *The Place That Has Never Been Wounded: Meditations* by Niall Breslin for musical meditations to accompany the reflections found in this book.

Available now on Audible and Spotify.

ISBN 978 1 399 83823 8

Find out more at https://www.johnmurraypress.co.uk

RAISING READERS
Books Build Bright Futures

Dear Reader,

We'd love your attention for one more page to tell you about the crisis in children's reading, and what we can all do.

Studies have shown that reading for fun is the **single biggest predictor of a child's future life chances** – more than family circumstance, parents' educational background or income. It improves academic results, mental health, wealth, communication skills, ambition and happiness.[1]

The number of children reading for fun is in rapid decline. Young people have a lot of competition for their time. In 2024, 1 in 10 children and young people in the UK aged 5 to 18 did not own a single book at home.[2]

Hachette works extensively with schools, libraries and literacy charities, but here are some ways we can all raise more readers:

- Reading to children for just 10 minutes a day makes a difference
- Don't give up if children aren't regular readers – there will be books for them!
- Visit bookshops and libraries to get recommendations
- Encourage them to listen to audiobooks
- Support school libraries
- Give books as gifts

There's a lot more information about how to encourage children to read on our website: **www.RaisingReaders.co.uk**

Thank you for reading.

---

[1] OECD, '21st-Century Readers: Developing Literacy Skills in a Digital World', 2021, https://www.oecd.org/en/publications/21st-century-readers_a83d84cb-en.html

[2] National Literacy Trust, 'Book Ownership in 2024', November 2024, https://literacytrust.org.uk/research-services/research-reports/book-ownership-in-2024